CYBER RISK AT SCALE: NATIONAL FRAMEWORKS, INFRASTRUCTURE PROTECTION, AND AI-DRIVEN THREAT DEFENSE

SHAIKH AHMED

&

SHAIKH IRFAN

notionpress.com

INDIA • SINGAPORE • MALAYSIA

ISBN
Paperback 979-8-90451-586-7
Hardcase 979-8-90451-587-4

CONTENTS

3. Critical Infrastructure Protection in a Hyperconnected World

4. AI-Driven Threat Detection and Intelligent Defense Systems

5. Future Directions in Cyber Risk Management

PREFACE

Cybersecurity is no longer just a technical discipline — it is a critical necessity in today's interconnected digital landscape. As organizations rapidly adopt cloud technologies and digital transformation, the complexity and scale of cyber threats continue to grow, demanding not only advanced tools but also deep practical expertise and real-world experience.

This book is written with the vision of simplifying complex cybersecurity concepts and making them accessible to both aspiring professionals and experienced practitioners. Drawing from over 14 years of hands-on industry experience in Data Loss Prevention (DLP), Identity & Access Management (IAM), Privileged Access Management (PAM), Security Operations (SOC), Incident Response, and Cloud Security, Shaikh Ahmed brings practical insights from working in highly regulated and large-scale enterprise environments.

Throughout this work, the focus is on real-world scenarios, practical implementations, and actionable strategies — from securing endpoints and cloud environments to managing identities, preventing data exfiltration, and responding to advanced threats. The goal is to bridge the gap between theoretical knowledge and practical execution.

Whether you are beginning your cybersecurity journey or advancing your career, this book aims to guide you with clarity, relevance, and purpose.

Dedication

We dedicate this work to our family, whose unwavering support, encouragement, and belief have been the foundation of this journey.

To our parents, for their sacrifices, guidance, and values that shaped who we are today.

And to every cybersecurity professional and learner committed to protecting the digital world — this work is for you.

ACKNOWLEDGEMENT

We would like to express our heartfelt gratitude to everyone who supported us throughout this journey.

First and foremost, we thank our family for their constant support, patience, and encouragement. Their belief in us has been the driving force behind completing this work.

We are deeply grateful to our mentors, colleagues, and industry leaders who have shared their knowledge, provided guidance, and inspired continuous growth. The experience gained through working with global organizations and complex cybersecurity environments has significantly contributed to the insights shared in this book.

Special thanks to the global cybersecurity community — researchers, practitioners, and innovators — whose continuous efforts in advancing security technologies and frameworks inspire professionals worldwide.

Finally, we extend our sincere thanks to our readers. Your passion for learning and commitment to securing the digital world motivate us to share our knowledge and experience

Chapter 1

THE EVOLUTION OF CYBER RISK IN THE DIGITAL AGE

1. OVERVIEW

The most ambiguous aspect of a cyber risk management strategy is the digital risk management role. A lot of corporate CISOs arė starting to plan and carry out a digital transformation project. A CISO may find it challenging to understand their job at this turning point, let alone where they will stand after the change.

The technology that a particular company uses creates digital risk. For this reason, A program for managing digital risks must be specific to the company. Gartner's approach for creating a digital risk management program is determined by the risks and the technology groups that businesses employ:

- A third party
- Social media
- On the go
- Large-scale data
- The Internet of Things
- The cloud

These new technologies are used by each sector and company, and the particular dangers they cause increase the difficulty of defining digital risk management in general. For those going through digital transformation, risk management is an ongoing activity. As a starting point, based on particular use cases, we will examine the common uses of these technologies and the related digital hazards.

2. UNDERSTANDING CYBER RISK AT SCALE

Cyber risk, also known as cybersecurity risk or cyber security risk, is defined as the likelihood that a threat, system flaw, or human activity will jeopardize the availability, confidentiality, or integrity of information systems, having an adverse effect on operations, finances, or reputation to the organization, making cyber risk a core enterprise risk concern for leadership and security teams alike. Put simply, if you're wondering what cybersecurity risk is, it's the possibility that a cyber event – whether caused by a mistake, a system flaw, or a malicious actor – will negatively affect the privacy, honesty, or integrity of your information and schemes.

Risks can come from anywhere: either outside from viruses, third-party providers with a lax security posture, or internal sabotage by rogue employees or careless security procedures like not routinely patching software.

One of the biggest and most worrisome threats of our time is the possibility of cyberattacks. Hackers are continuously looking for every weakness they can exploit with the aid of automated bot armies. A network invasion can occur with just a small weakness in an organization's defenses, dramatically increasing your overall cyber-attack risk and the likelihood of a serious incident.

Since the majority of cyberattacks, these days aim to gain organizational data, data breaches are a major cyberattack risk. How would you feel if a malevolent hacker had access to all of your company's sensitive data, including your clients' private information? It's somewhat unsettling, isn't it?

Businesses run the risk of breaking cybersecurity and data privacy laws by disclosing private client information.

Types of cyber risks to manage

Not all cyber risks look the same, and not all of them come from hackers. A strong cyber risk management strategy accounts for a wide range of threats, from technical failures to human error to third-party dependencies. The following is a list of some of the most prevalent risk categories experienced by most organizations today:

- **Operational risks:** They involve system outage, bugs and configuration errors that interfere with day-to-day operations. A minor issue, such as a missed patch or an expired certificate, is enough to put business-important systems down.
- **Insider threats:** Once the employees, contractors, or vendors get access to sensitive data, they may abuse it either deliberately or unintentionally. Emails misaddressed, file sharing that is insecure, and use of shadow IT applications are all invitations to leaks.
- **Risks based on credentials:** Phishing attacks, re-use of passwords, or leaked logins in the dark web may provide attackers with access to internal tools. Credential protection is now more important than ever, as there are more SaaS logins and remote users.
- **Regulatory and compliance risks:** The inability to comply with standards such as the General Data Protection Regulation, the Payment Card Industry Data Security Standard, or the Health Insurance Portability and Accountability Act may cause legal fines and a decrease in reputation. These risks can be described as a result of data not being classified properly, the absence of audit logs, or access controls.
- **Third-party risks:** Integrations and vendors increase your digital footprint, but increase your exposure, too. A poor connection in your supply chain is capable of exposing weak links that you do not have direct control over.

The first step to managing cyber risks is to identify what kind of threats you are experiencing- and develop an appropriate defense in infrastructure, people, and processes. To the owners of SaaS business applications, it is also a chance to become a subject matter expert worth keeping since they can assist the CISOs, GRC teams and InfoSec leaders to comprehend how these risks are applied within your SaaS context.

By recommending configurations and enhancements that align with corporate security policies, you not only strengthen the organization's defenses but also build expertise that can boost your own value.

What should a cyber risk management strategy include?

Guesswork is not the way to go when it comes to a strong cyber risk strategy. Instead, you need to follow a clear process that every part of your organization can adopt and support.

A simple recommendation of a three-step interactive process for SaaS owners to understand when it comes to their strategy: Understand, Protect, and Monitor. That should be the foundation of your cyber risk management strategy.

With those foundational goal posts in mind, you can also refer to the NIST Cybersecurity Framework. One of the most widely adopted approaches is Govern, Classify, Defend, Sense, Reply, and Improve, which are the six purposes delineated in the NIST CSF. Every function aims at minimizing exposure and makes security a part of daily operations rather than a rush at the end of the day.

1. **Govern**

   Establish regulations, roles and duties. Governance refers to the process of defining decision-making on cybersecurity. As an example, who assesses the risk profile of a new tool when it is introduced? Who owns the data it accesses? These guardrails are necessary in order to prevent good tech from blindly creating blind spots.

2. **Identify**

   Get an inventory of your systems, assets, data and suppliers and know which are most essential. Security Center assists in this part as it assists with risk scoring and prioritization based on data, thus you can quickly see where attention is required initially. An example of this is that one organization, say a healthcare organization, could have patient records as a priority, whereas the other organization, say a retailer, could have payment processing systems as one of its priorities. It is to be aware of what you are defending and why. Identify, as defined under the NIST CSF, also refers to seeking methods on how to enhance policies and practices in all six functions and forms a heavier baseline to all other elements of your security plan.

3. **Protect**

   Implement protection against threats. This consists of identity and access control, encryption, and user authentication. Data security and privacy are equally important - the Principle of Least Privilege implies that a user should have only the accessible access. Security Center automatically finds suspicious permissions and makes it easier and faster maintenance of the least privileged access. The adoption of MFA can be used to prevent unauthorized logins to the user accounts, particularly during hybrid or remote working environments.

4. **Detect**

   Real-time threat monitoring prevents the detection and identification of abnormal conduct in time before it turns into a major security event. Detect as a component of the NIST CSF also involves analysis of adverse events - exploring suspicious activity to determine its extent and possible effect. Early identification and analysis provide the teams with additional time to take action before it is too late.

5. **Respond**

   When something does go wrong, a quick and systematic response restricts damage. Respond is also covered under the NIST CSF, and it covers incident analysis and reporting, which implies the ability to record the facts of what occurred and disseminate the appropriate information to the appropriate stakeholders. These activities usually require a lot of reliance on Salesforce Event Monitoring, which offers the information required to comprehend the event, record the response, and satisfy the reporting. Availability of incident response playbooks, escalation tracks and communication schemes can make a crisis a solvable problem. It is not prevention but the reduction of the consequences of all attacks.

6. **Recover**

   Since breaches of data are a when rather than an if, rapid recovery will keep your business going. Recovery plans are a must, regardless of whether it is to restore access to applications or retrieve the necessary data.

   The combination of six principles gives a basis of proactive management of cyber risk. They provide security, IT and compliance leaders with a common process that is flexible enough to fit the industry of any type and designed to suit a world that never stops discovering new forms of threats.

Best cyber risk management systems.

It is evident that the risk profile is not the same in every organization or field. Others are run with strict industry laws, whereas some can still value speed and scalability more than the conventional security model. The selection of an appropriate cyber risk management framework allows its protection to be adapted to the needs of your business without reinventing the wheel.

You may build and apply your own framework or use industry frameworks and approaches, like NIST or other models. The following are the ways in which some of the most popular models can be used to support various elements of the cyber risk strategy:

1. **Nation World Economic Forum (WEF) Cyber Resilience Framework.**

   WEF is designed to address the needs of businesses that have to function within highly interconnected environments and is more concerned with resilience, as opposed to defense. It describes six fundamental principles:

   - Embed cybersecurity into business strategy
   - Engage leadership and shareholders

- Promote a philosophy of cybersecurity mindfulness
- Ensure internal and external collaboration
- Foster systemic resilience across supply chains
- Get ready to recover and carry on.

The distinction of this model is that it focuses on common responsibility. It acknowledges the fact that a single organization cannot reduce cyber threats single-handedly, in particular, when third-party collaborators and international infrastructure are at play.

2. **Other risk management systems.**

These other options provide viable advice on how to develop a risk-aware security program depending on your industry and level of maturity:

- **Communication: Center of Internet Security (CIS) Top 20 controls:** A list of defensive actions with priorities, which are best suited to organizations that wish to begin with high-impact basics, such as asset inventory, access control and audit logging.
- **ISO/IEC 27001/27002:** An information security management system (ISMS) that is globally accepted and is commonly applied by companies in an attempt to address international compliance standards.
- **Factor Analysis of Information Risk (FAIR):** A financial risk measure quantitative model, which can assist business leaders in determining cybersecurity spending as they do with other risks.
- **Payment Card Industry Data Security Standard (PCI DSS):** The business needs this requirement because it processes credit card payments. The system protects payment environments through security measures against both data theft and fraud.

- **Health Insurance Portability and Accountability Act (HIPAA):** The health care segment uses HIPAA procedures to define methods for safeguarding patient information and achieving required privacy standards through electronic medical systems. Different frameworks provide distinct approaches for managing cyber risk because they focus on different aspects of their respective domains. The key is selecting one that fits with how you operate and where your risks.

Use-Cases for Risk Management in Digital Transformation

1. **Third-Party Risk Management**

   The area of digital risk management most directly related to supply chain risk management is third-party digital risk management. It represents the company's evolution from an individual to an ecosystem. With its increasing reliance on suppliers and focus on its key differentiators and revenue generators, the modern business resembles an ecosystem due to the increased outsourcing of ancillary jobs and technologies.

   Third-party digital risks can be addressed and reduced using frameworks that are comparable to those used in the rest of the supply chain because they are the most similar to supply-chain risk management. The intricacy of third-party digital risk appears when your vendor risk team enquires about the technologies that vendors are utilizing as part of a digital transformation. In those situations, evaluate your digital supply chain using the recommendations for the other five technologies and paradigms.

2. **Social Media**

   The dangers related to an organization's reputation is at risk from a variety of social media activities, including phishing, account hacking, and hashtag and handle imitation, making social media risk perhaps the easiest component of digital risk management.

   To put it briefly, how can potential clients and existing clients expect you to protect sensitive data, much less concentrate on a proactive approach to digital risk management, if your security staff is unable to safeguard your social media accounts and digital communication channels?

3. **Mobile**

Although mobile risk varies widely, managing the organization's rules and procedures is crucial for digital transformation. CISOs and security directors need to examine how their company employs mobile devices to identify the associated digital risks.

System libraries, firmware, OS versions, security update versions, device configuration, and system settings to find security holes, device vulnerabilities, and dubious or malicious behavior are the common dangers that mobile devices face, according to Gartner. Because digitizing corporate activities can result in continually changing goals for digital security risk management, risk management in digital transformation is a significant challenge for many business models.

Today's mobile devices should be handled as such because they are more similar to the computers on our desks. Our mobile devices frequently hold just as much, if not more, data than our desktop computers. When evaluating the digital risks connected to mobile devices in their approach to digital risk management, information security leaders—from CIOs to CISOs to Chief Risk Officers—must be closely examined in order to reduce the probability and impact of a cyberattack.

4. **Big Data**

Almost all consumers and company executives are fascinated by artificial intelligence, machine learning, and big data. A CISO's digital risk strategy may be built around big data technologies. The dangers of big data solutions have long been discussed. In contrast, serious data hazards are not as important as other aspects of digital risk management readily apparent.

3. HISTORICAL DEVELOPMENT OF CYBER THREATS

Let's start with some basic information about cybersecurity. Cybersecurity is safeguarding computer networks, programs, systems, and data against cyber threats, unauthorized access, damage, and theft. The processes and tools that support this effort are likewise related to cybersecurity.

Cybersecurity consists of various elements, including as but not limited to:

- **Network security:** First and foremost, safeguarding networks and their infrastructure from disruptions, intrusions, and attacks. Interruption discovery and anticipation schemes, virtual private networks (VPNs), and firewalls.
- **Information security:** Emphasizes safeguarding an organization's data accessibility, confidentiality, and integrity. Examples include putting in place safeguards like data backups, access limits, and encryption.
- **Application Security:** The process of securing packages and claims starts with locating vulnerabilities that attackers can exploit to achieve their goals. The system uses regular software updates together with patches as its protective measures against security threats.
- **Endpoint Security:** The protection of specific gadgets such as PCs, tablets, and smartphones. Security solutions include things like mobile device management (MDM) technology, antivirus software, and endpoint detection and response (EDR) systems.

As one might anticipate, cybersecurity is a fairly broad term that includes incident response and management, security governance, user access to systems and networks, and security awareness training.

Let's examine significant occurrences, paradigm shifts, and the now-familiar cat and mouse game between security specialists and hostile actors from the early days of computers, when security was practically an afterthought (if a consideration at all) to the current era of sophisticated cyber threats is essentially an endless battle.

1940 – 1950s

Cybersecurity's history began in the 1940s. More precisely, the first all-purpose electronic digital computer was the Electronic Numerical Integrator and Computer, or ENIAC, introduced in 1945.

These machineries were big, loud, and—above all—extremely uncommon. They were mostly employed in military and scientific computations. In actuality, there were only a handful worldwide. To be honest, the majority of people were unaware that they even existed.

Many individuals continue to speculate about what networks might look like in the future, despite the fact that they were still absent in the 1940s. Therefore, even though there are currently no links between devices, John von Neumann and other theorists were already considering the possible appearance of a virus. His primary concept? The potential for a mechanical organism to multiply and spread to new hosts. The fundamentals of virus theory were established twenty years before his paper, Theory of Self-Reproducing Automata, was published in the 1960s.

The first instances of hacking appeared in the 1950s. In particular, the capacity to manipulate telephone protocols, or "phone phreaking," is not as entertaining as it seems. The primary goal was to make it possible for people to make calls at a lower cost or for free (we're getting ahead somewhat, but did you know that the founders of the enormous tech giant Apple, Steve Jobs and Steve Wozniak, effectively started the business in the 1970s following a prosperous period in which they built and sold phone phreaking equipment?

However, contemporary computers were developed in the 1940s. Large mainframe computers and the start of the digital age can be seen here. These costly devices were mostly employed in the military and scientific fields. The idea of networked computers was not commonly accepted, and security methods were comparatively simple.

1960 – 1970s

Computers remained quite large and costly during the 1960s, which is most known not for technology but rather due to the numerous social and cultural changes that were brought about. In actuality, however, the first hackers emerged in this decade. Now, the 1960s saw a wide range of hacker activity from that of today.

The primary goal of these older computer hacking operations was to access specific systems. IBM discovered potential weaknesses through this procedure, which we now often refer to as "user testing." Thus, security measures were already a source of concern.

However, the environment of cyber threats was still developing in the 1960s. Furthermore, there was no awareness of cyberattacks as we know them today. The hardware's physical security and preventing unauthorized access to the restricted computer resources remained the main concerns. But the concept of cybersecurity as a separate sector has not yet materialized, and there were no recognized security protocols.

The 1970s are often linked to disco, bell-bottom trousers and presidential scandals. For some, the cybersecurity sector truly took off throughout this decade. Given that the Advanced Research Projects Agency Network (ARPANET) was established in September 1969, this should not be shocking. The ARPANET was the first packet-switched network in history, established at the beginning of the decade, and served as the cornerstone for the Internet.

Facilitating Interaction and the sharing of resources between institutions and scholars was the aim of ARPANET. It is untrue to say that ARPANET was motivated by the need for a robust, decentralized system that could withstand nuclear attacks.

"The ARPANET was not started to create a Command-and-Control System that would survive a nuclear attack, as many now claim," said former ARPANET director Charles Herzfeld in an interview with Ars Technica. It was obviously a critical military need to develop such a system, but ARPA was not tasked with doing so; Actually, if we had tried to do so, we would have been met with severe condemnation. Rather, we were dissatisfied with the lack. Considering the nation's huge, potent research computers and the reality that many academics who ought to have access to them were geographically far away, which prompted the construction of the ARPANET.

1980 – 1990s

The 1980s, which saw the emergence of Reaganomics, glam metal, and hip-hop music, were certainly the decade of prominent attacks on public and private establishments. During this period, computers also became more individualized. As a result, there was a discernible shift in favor of different systems.

Bulletin Board Systems (BBS) were commonly used in computers in the 1980s. This widely used technique allowed users to use a modem to connect their personal computers to a host system. As sharing became easier, security concerns therefore surged. This site prominently exhibits a variety of viruses and malware, including the notorious Brain virus (1986), which infected IBM PC-compatible systems, and the Elk Cloner virus (1982), which targeted Apple II computers. The first widespread malware epidemic was caused by the Morris Worm to the public by Robert Tappan Morris in 1988.

In 1983, the Domain Name System, or DNS, was developed to facilitate internet navigation. Even so, the primary method of controlling access was passwords; security procedures were still frequently inadequate. For government organizations, which understood the value of information system security, the situation was quite different. For instance, National Security Decision Directive 145, issued by President Ronald Reagan in 1983, addressed computer and telecommunications system security.

The first ransomware attack also occurred in the 1980s; it was supplied to attendees of the World Health Organization's AIDS conference via floppy disc and was cruelly named AIDS or Aids Info Disc, considering the epidemic at the time. Joseph L. Popp, the program's creator, was detained and accused of several counts of blackmail.

In a nutshell, the 1980s were a time of innovation, exploration, and early connectedness. Out of curiosity or challenge, people began genuinely looking into and exploiting vulnerabilities. But cyber espionage also began to appear during this time. For example, in 1986, Marcus Hess, a German, used ARPANET to breach government computers. He gained access to around 400 military computers in a matter of minutes.

This decade is notable not just for the rise of grunge music and "The Simpsons," but also for the rapid expansion of the Internet, the ongoing development of personal computers, and the cybersecurity sector.

The 1990s witnessed both the commercialization of the web and the ongoing development of digital technologies. However, as we indicated, cybersecurity issues increased along with Internet usage.

For instance, new types of cyberthreats, such as the popularity Using IRC and online communities like America Online (AOL) resulted in the rise of social engineering, distributed denial-of-service (DDoS) assaults, and illegal access.

Additionally, since Microsoft Windows had become the most widely used operating system for personal computers, hackers focused more on it (how else could Microsoft persuade some "Friends" stars to host their Windows 95 user manual?).

Malware, including viruses and worms, mostly targeted Windows systems because of their widespread use. Many businesses started creating firewalls as a defense in reaction to it.

Since its founding in 1990, the Electronic Frontier Foundation has grown to become a well-known advocate for civil liberties and digital rights. In addition to promoting crucial public discussions about the required rules, the Electronic Frontier Foundation was instrumental in resolving legal issues pertaining to cybersecurity protection. And EFF is still working today.

2000s: Breaches, Clouds, and All the Mobile Devices

Increased connectedness resulted from the widespread use of broadband internet during the 2000s, a decade characterized by the iPod's popularity, Middle East hostilities, and the Great Recession.

Although this provided us with in addition to making the internet quicker and more dependable, it expanded the target area for cyberattacks. When you combine it as online banking and e-commerce have grown, you'll find that a variety of new cybersecurity problems have emerged, including identity theft and financial data hacking, and phishing attacks directed to the sensitive information of users.

Another development that followed the 2000s was the influx of advanced malware, such as worms, viruses, and trojans. Two prominent examples of worms that exploited vulnerabilities in Windows systems are Code Red and Nimda.

Like the augmented use of mobile devices, the issue of mobile security has increased as well. Smartphone data leaks, illegal access, and mobile malware have become serious cybersecurity concerns.

Simultaneously, the implementation of cloud computing came with a set of security issues in terms of the shared responsibility paradigm, access control, and data protection.

Some of the most well-known data breaches were observed during this period, including those of the larger organizations and governmental bodies. Such cases as the TJX data breach (2007) highlighted the necessity of effective cybersecurity practices.

Today, the necessity for cybersecurity systems has resulted in the development of a strong cybersecurity market. The market for intrusion detection systems, firewalls, antivirus software, and other cybersecurity products in the 2000s grew.

2010s: New Leaks, More Destruction

The 2010s have seen a dramatic change in the cyber threat. Even more spectacular hacks, paradigm shifts, and the shift from data theft to physical destruction have occurred in this decade.

The worm known as Stuxnet was one such example, as it ushered in a new dawn in the evolution of cyber warfare (it was presumed to be an operation undertaken by the U.S. and Israel and targeted nuclear installations in Iran).

It was also during this period that Snowden leaks unveiled a global surveillance system. It resulted in the proliferation of cyber-espionage and created foreign intelligence-gathering activities by different nations.

The other new trends in technology and cybersecurity emerged during the decade. Specifically, artificial intelligence and machine learning started to be applied to cyber defense, where the former was utilized to detect and stop malware as well as trigger recoveries, as well.

Large-scale information leaks, economically driven online crime and malicious malware made a lot of systems useless during the 2010s. Cyber-espionage activities and devastating cyberattacks also increased exponentially throughout the decade, which underscores the need to fight them.

Cybersecurity Today

Cyber threats have now become more advanced in the past few years. Both nation-state-backed cyber activities and advanced persistent threats (APTs) employ efficient techniques that can compromise systems without being discovered. Unfortunately, ransomware attacks have also increased in frequency and pose a serious threat to key infrastructure, government agencies, and enterprises. Additionally, we have sophisticated social engineering attacks like deep fake technologies.

Artificial intelligence and machine learning technologies are increasingly being used in cybersecurity, and energy, healthcare, and transportation systems are all becoming more susceptible to attack. These skills improve threat recognition, automate reply processes, and offer active defense against new attacks. On top of that, the growing use of cloud computing makes it easy to understand how security must be of chief concern (World Economic Forum, 2025)Artificial Intelligence and Cybersecurity: Balancing Risks and Rewards.

There are more complex challenges to be faced in the future, including the spread of the Internet of Things (IoT) or how cryptographic methods will be affected by quantum computing. Therefore, in order to have a truly practical and cooperative strategy to cybersecurity, we must ignore all of the lessons learned from the past. One that is distinguished by constant alertness, learning, and the creation of creative solutions.

4. ECONOMIC AND GEOPOLITICAL IMPACTS OF CYBER INCIDENTS

Not only have the cyber-attacks tried to disrupt the technical processes, but they have also become an important economic and geopolitical threat to the countries, institutions and the global economies. Losses of billions of dollars of operational disruption, data theft and recovery of the financial institutions, critical infrastructure and multinational corporations can be experienced due to the huge cyber-attacks. Besides causing direct financial losses, cyber occurrences will also cause indirect economic losses to the economy in terms of loss of consumer confidence, market instability, fines, and reputation in the long-term. One advanced cyber-attack could pose a threat to the entire economic stability of an industry, even though the global trade, financial systems, and supply chains are progressively becoming reliant on digital infrastructure.

Cyber events have turned into a weapon of strategic competition among nation-states, geopolitically speaking. The offensive and defensive cyber capabilities are now being used by governments as an everyday weapon in their national security strategies. Government-sponsored cyber operations are normally used in espionage missions, intellectual property theft, political influence and havoc campaigns against the infrastructure of the antagonizing nations. Such activities blur cybercrime, cyberwar and spy wars. As a result, cyber events can enhance the state of relations between states, lead to counteractions and influence the course of international relations, especially in cases of attribution towards the interference of a state.

Better yet, the interdependent nature of the international digital environment enhances the geopolitical implications of cyber-incidents. The spillover effects can be noticeable in a number of countries and sectors after being attacked in the chain of supply, cloud service providers or cross-border financial networks. International coordination of cybersecurity, regulation, and information exchange activities by the governments and international bodies are emerging as one of the priorities in order to mitigate the systemic risks. Enhancing global cyber resilience is now a critical challenge in the protection of digital assets as well as in ensuring the economic stability, national sovereignty, and international security in a more digitized world.

The impacts on the economy

1. The global cost

Since almost every kind of illicit activity now occurs online, beyond cybercrime, the breadth of criminal activities on the internet has significantly expanded. A senior British official claims that cybercrimes account for more than half of all crimes reported in the UK. We created a more precise definition that only accounts for the expense of thieves obtaining unauthorized access in order to eliminate the overall cost of all detrimental internet activities on a targeted victim's computer or network. Based on this description, the following elements of the cost of cybercrime have been identified:

- Damage to private corporate information and intellectual property.
- Stolen personal information is often the root cause of financial crimes and online fraud.
- Financial manipulation includes financial swindling, such as gaining early access to the financial reports of publicly traded companies or sensitive business information on possible acquisitions.
- A decline in confidence in online activities and a disturbance in service or output. Although ransomware poses a serious risk to companies, it can also result in serious issues with service disruptions.
- Covering the cost of recovering from cyberattacks, as well as network security and cyber insurance.

Cybercrime has cost tens of billions to even a trillion dollars. Numerous approaches and inadequate data are to blame for this. Economic history study is best suited for predicting the costs of cybercrime because the data is occasionally inconsistent and partial. According to CSIS, the estimated $600 billion global cost of cybercrime is the target of this modeling study.

2. **Estimation issues**

Accurately estimating the cost of cybercrime presents a number of challenges. It is more challenging for victims to come forward and for the government to gather statistics in some nations since different businesses have varied reporting regulations. Only 13% of cybercrimes are recorded in the UK, according to data from that nation.

To exacerbate the situation, a lot of organizations that have been victims of cybercrime choose not to come forward. National estimates are infamously inaccurate, and at the national level, obtaining trustworthy statistics is still difficult. Underreporting is the biggest barrier to accurately calculating the price of cybercrime. To reduce accountability and harm to the brand, just a small portion of losses are disclosed.

Determining the actual cost of consumers avoiding online transactions is another problem because they are afraid of falling victim to cybercrime. There are indications that this may be changing, but the attraction of digital technology is still too great for individuals and companies to give it up.

Lastly, our cost estimate has the drawback of providing governments with the entire cost as opposed to the expense borne by specific companies or customers. The uneven distribution of victims is not taken into consideration. For instance, if a nation has ten enterprises and loses $100 annually due to cybercrime, the average cost per company is $10. Two businesses lose $50, while the other eight businesses either lose nothing or very little, depending on the actual distribution. Organizations suffer losses in different ways, and some might not even be aware that they have been compromised.

3. **Financial cybercrime**

Highly skilled cybercriminals still frequently attack banks. For over ten years, this has been the situation. The burden of preventing financial organizations are disproportionately affected by overt theft and online fraud. According to one report, bank executives saw cybercrime as a Banks invest three times as much in cyber security as non-financial businesses due to the "systematic" threat to financial stability.

Nation-states are the biggest source of cybercrime due to their enormous financial resources, information access, and immunity from law enforcement. According to the CSIS, the countries that hack financial institutions the most frequently are Iran, North Korea, and Russia. China is still the country that conducts the most espionage. Iran's desire to use coercive influence is demonstrated by the distributed denial-of-service (DDoS) attack on prominent US organizations.

Whether they are employed by the local governments, this area is home to several of the most active hackers in the world. If these nations don't change, cybercrime will remain a global issue.

4. **Ransomware**

What caused this quick growth? When ransomware first emerged, victims were sent floppy CDs containing questionnaires asking them to rate their risk of contracting AIDS. The program on the disc had locked their PCs, so they had to wire $189 in cash to a Panama P.O. box. Many things have changed since then; the artisanal use of ransomware has been surpassed by the virus's global dissemination. When ransomware attacks first appeared in 2015, the criminal organizations that developed the programs were usually responsible for carrying them out. In 2016 alone, 70 new families of ransomware products were released, which doubled the number of new products from 2012 to 2015.

Solutions for Reducing the Impact

Terrorism and organized crime will probably be combined into one threat in the upcoming cyberattacks. There is a growing expectation that businesses will safeguard everything they produce as the Internet of Things (IoT) connects everything. Both small firms and multibillion-dollar organizations lose money, data, and public trust as a result of a violation. There are several approaches to combat the cybercrime epidemic, such as:

- Consistent implementation of fundamental Ongoing investment in defensive technology, from mobile devices to the cloud, is essential, as are security measures like regular software updates, patches, and open security designs. Preventing cybercrime doesn't necessarily require the most advanced safeguards. Businesses bear the brunt of this responsibility, along with consumers.
- The corporate community and foreign law enforcement agencies must work together more to combat cybercrime. This calls for the growth of agency resources in developing nations as well as additional resources for investigations.
- It is possible to enhance current processes, like the Mutual Legal Assistance Treaty (MLAT). To look into cybercrime or collect evidence using MLATs, governments might ask one another for help. MLATs had to be modified or replaced because they were ineffective prior to the Internet.
- More standardization (threat data) and collaboration. Adopting cybersecurity standards would improve security in important industries like finance.
- Why do countries with weak cybercrime laws have higher rates of cybercrime, which causes issues for those countries' neighbors?
- However, the Budapest Pact—a formal pact against cybercrime—has made some headway despite opposition from Russia and other nations. Russia claims that the agreement is excessively intrusive and could not be motivated to curb Russian criminal organizations. They assert that they are unable to sign the treaty because they did not participate in the negotiations. If new conventions aren't agreed on soon, there won't be any progress in reducing cybercrime.

- Lastly, the international community has to put pressure on Countries that have turned into safe havens for cybercrime to change their laws and collaborate with international law enforcement. Governments that fail are therefore subject to fines and other repercussions. North Korea's sanctions and Russia have run out, and in order to deal with these nations, new punishments that are both severe and reversible must be created.

In conclusion, threats and investments will continue to target the cybersecurity field. It will be more important than ever to possess security teams capable of preventing intrusions, anticipating attacks, and responding fast to newly identified vulnerabilities. To properly prevent and combat cybercrime, a global strategy is required. Although a company's financial collapse is never fun, its long-term brand reputation and capacity to recover will depend on how well (or poorly) it handles a financial crisis.

Why Geopolitical Conflicts Translate into Cyber Threats

Modern conflicts extend beyond physical borders. Nations now deploy cyber operations to:

- Disrupt critical infrastructure
- Steal intellectual property
- Conduct spying
- Influence markets
- Target financial systems
- Undermine economic stability

When tensions escalate globally, cyberattacks often increase in volume and sophistication. Indian businesses with global exposure, foreign partnerships, or cross-border data flows become indirect targets.

1. **Rise of State-Sponsored Attacks**

   Cyber campaigns are frequently initiated by the state through geopolitical confrontations. These attacks may target:

- Banking institutions
- Energy providers
- Telecom networks
- Defense contractors
- Government-linked enterprises

Even private businesses can be targeted if they are part of strategic supply chains

State-sponsored attacks are typically:

- Highly coordinated
- Persistent
- Well-funded
- Advanced in technique

Traditional defenses may not be sufficient.

2. **Supply Chain Vulnerabilities**

Indian companies are becoming dependent on:

- Global cloud providers
- International SaaS vendors
- Offshore development teams
- Hardware imported from abroad

Geopolitical variability can:

- Compromise vendor security
- Increase third-party breaches
- Disrupt critical updates or patches
- Introduce malware into supply chains

The vendor risk governance will be critical when it comes to global conflicts.

3. **Ransomware as a Political Tool**

   Ransomware attacks in recent years have been associated with geopolitical reasons. Attackers may:

   - Target organizations in specific regions
   - Disrupt operations during sensitive periods
   - Leak politically sensitive data

   Ransomware campaigns may spike during international crises, elections, or sanctions. Such trends should be expected by Indian firms that run their business internationally.

4. **More Phishing and Disinformation Campaigns.**

   Social engineering and misinformation are driven by geopolitical wars. Attackers exploit:

   - Breaking news events
   - Military tensions
   - Trade sanctions
   - Political announcements

   Phishing emails disguised as urgent geopolitical updates often bypass employee suspicion. Deepfake technologies further amplify this threat.

5. **Regulatory & Compliance Pressure**

   During geopolitical instability, regulators may tighten:

   - Incident reporting timelines
   - Cyber resilience requirements
   - Cross-border data transfer rules
   - Vendor security standards

   Indian regulators expect businesses to maintain operational resilience regardless of global tensions. Compliance lapses during crises are not excused.

6. **Financial Market Targeting**

   Financial institutions and fintech companies face elevated risk during global tensions. Cyberattacks may aim to:

   - Manipulate trading systems
   - Access financial records
   - Cause market disruption
   - Undermine investor confidence

   Indian BFSI organizations must maintain continuous monitoring and incident readiness.

7. **Critical Infrastructure & Strategic Sectors at Risk**

   Energy, telecom, manufacturing, logistics, and healthcare sectors are especially vulnerable during geopolitical conflicts.

   Disruptions in these sectors can:

   - Affect supply chains
   - Impact national stability
   - Create cascading economic effects

Businesses in these sectors must elevate their cybersecurity posture.

5. CYBER WARFARE AND STATE-SPONSORED ATTACKS

Cyberwarfare is occasionally used to describe a cyberattack or a string of attacks directed at a nation. It has the capacity to destroy civilian and governmental infrastructure and impede vital operations, endangering the state and possibly leading to fatalities.

However, there is disagreement among cybersecurity specialists regarding the precise definition of cyberwarfare. The US Department of Defense (DoD) admits that there is a risk to national security from malicious Internet use, but it does not define cyberwarfare precisely. Cyberwarfare is viewed by some as a potentially fatal cyberattack.

Cyberwarfare usually entails a country-state launching cyberattacks on another, but occasionally terrorist groups Such Non-state actors launch attacks in an effort to further the objectives of a hostile nation. There isn't a formal, standard definition for what constitutes an act of war in a cyberattack, despite the fact that there have been several documented cases of cyberwarfare in recent years.

State-sponsored cyberattacks are malevolent online activities carried out by hackers who are either directly or indirectly supported by a government. Whether they entail espionage, upsetting enemies, or swaying public opinion, these attacks are usually intended to further national goals. Because they are less expensive, simpler to carry out than conventional military operations, and offer a high level of plausible deniability, cyberattacks are a desirable instrument for state actors.

Categories of Cyber Warfare Operations

- **Espionage: R**efers to keeping an eye on other nations in order to steal secrets. This could entail using spear phishing or botnets to breach vulnerable computer systems in order to collect private information.
- **Sabotage:** Government agencies must evaluate the dangers of compromising sensitive data. Information can be stolen, destroyed, or used by terrorists or hostile nations through insider threats, such as irate or negligent workers or public servants with ties to the nation that is attacking.
- **Attacks that cause a denial of service (DoS):** By flooding a website with fictitious requests and making it process them, denial-of-service (DoS) assaults stop legitimate users from accessing it. This kind of assault can be used to interfere with vital systems and operations and prevent people, military personnel, security specialists, or research groups from accessing crucial websites.
- **Grid for Power:** Attackers have the ability to physically injure individuals, interfere with infrastructure, and destroy vital systems by attacking the electrical grid. Attacks on the electrical grid have

the ability to interfere with communication and make services like text messaging and communication unusable.

- **Attacks using Propaganda:** Attempts to influence the beliefs and attitudes of those who reside in or defend a particular nation. Propaganda can be used to propagate false information to undermine public confidence, reveal embarrassing facts, or build alliances with adversaries.
- **Economic Upheaval:** Attempts to influence the beliefs and attitudes of those who reside in or defend a particular nation. Propaganda can be used to propagate false information to undermine public confidence, reveal embarrassing facts, or build alliances with adversaries.
- **Unexpected Assaults:** These are the digital counterparts of Pearl Harbor and 9/11. In order to weaken the enemy's defenses, the attacker intends to launch a tremendous assault for which they are unprepared. In the context of hybrid warfare, this could be done to set the stage for a physical assault.

Strategic Motivations Behind Cyber Warfare

- **Military:** Gaining control of important aspects of an enemy nation's internet is advantageous to the armed forces. A successful hack might secure what would have otherwise been an expensive victory by bringing an opponent nation's soldierly to its knees.
- **Civil:** Attacks on a nation's civic infrastructure have an immediate effect on its citizens. This could hurt the opponent politically by inciting fear or inciting a revolt against the government.
- **Hacktivism:** Hackers who use cyberattacks to further an ideology are known as hacktivists. Hacktivists can engage in cyberwarfare by spreading misinformation or chasing mysteries and then making them public. Hackers are able to prevent support from other nations by undermining an opponent's reputation on the international scene.

- **Generation of income:** Cyberwarfare "soldiers" may launch heinous assaults in order to profit financially. They may be compensated for their services if they work for the government. They may also take money for themselves and jeopardize a financial institution's security.
- **Nonprofit studies:** Nonprofit research frequently produces incredibly useful data that a nation might use to address a pressing issue. For instance, cyberwarfare may be used to steal information on a vaccine that one country is developing and another already has.

Examples of Cyber Warfare Operations

- **Stuxnet Virus:** A malware known as Stuxnet targeted Iran's nuclear program. It is one of the most advanced cyberattacks ever. The malware targeted data-collecting and supervisory control systems and propagated through infected Universal Serial Bus devices. According to the majority of reports, Iran's capacity to produce nuclear weapons was severely harmed by the attack.
- **Sony Pictures Hack:** Following the Sony Pictures faced criticism after the movie "The Interview," which had an unflattering portrayal of Kim Jong Un, was released. Hackers from the North Korean government are blamed for the attack. Code, encryption techniques, and data erasure techniques comparable to those used in earlier North Korean malware attacks were found by the FBI.
- **Bronze Soldier:** The Bronze Soldier statue, a representation of the Soviet Union, was relocated by Estonia in 2007 from a neighboring military cemetery to the heart of Tallinn, the country's capital. In the months that followed, Estonia was the target of several serious cyberattacks. Massive denial of service (DoS) attacks overwhelmed Estonian banks, media outlets, and government websites, bringing them down.
- **Fancy Bear:** According to CrowdStrike, a Russian organized hacking outfit, Fancy Bear targeted Ukrainian artillery and rocket forces between 2014 and 2016. Because the D-30 Howitzer artillery

regiment used an infected Android application to handle aiming data, the infection spread.

- The X-Agent malware was present in the app that Ukrainian officers often used. In what is regarded as a highly successful attack, about 80% of Ukraine's D-30s were destroyed. Howitzers.
- **Enemies of Qatar:** In 2018, American Republican fundraiser Elliott Broody filed a lawsuit against the Qatari government, claiming that it had stolen and revealed his emails in an effort to defame him. He was purportedly viewed by the Qataris as a roadblock to their advancement in Washington.

The lawsuit claims that the brother of the Qatari Emir and other members of the nation's leadership planned a cyberwarfare campaign. The same terrorists targeted 1,200 persons, many of whom were recognized as "enemies of Qatar," including high-ranking officials from Bahrain, Saudi Arabia, Egypt, and the United Arab Emirates.

Operational Mechanisms of State-Sponsored Attacks

There are several ways that governments use cyber capabilities. They can surreptitiously support independent hacker organizations or hire hackers directly through military units and intelligence agencies. Since it is challenging to immediately link an attack to a government, this type of indirect financing allows states to credibly deny that an attack was carried out by the government. These cyber units engage in a variety of illegal acts, including:

- **Espionage:** This is the unlawful acquisition of political information, corporate trade secrets, or classified government information.
- **Disruption of key infrastructure:** Undermining an adversary's economic and defense capabilities by attacking essential services such as power systems, the financial sector, and communication routes.
- **Disinformation:** Using online channels to divide societies, affect public opinion, and influence voters.

- **Building cyber defenses:** attacking to ascertain the adversary's ability to recognize and manage cyber threats, thereby exposing vulnerabilities that could be exploited in the future.

Evolution of State-Sponsored Cyber Operations

The goal of state-sponsored cyberwarfare, which dates back to the early days of computing, is intelligence gathering. For example, the Soviet Union and the United States engaged in cyberwarfare in the 1960s and 1970s to get access to classified material in the country of origin.

The rise of hackers and the development of the first computer viruses marked a watershed in the 1980s. The Morris worm and other significant cyberattacks on the internet in 1988 marked the beginning of the threat of cyberwarfare. The next ten years saw a rise in cyber espionage as countries like China and Russia began using hacking techniques to obtain private information from other countries.

As the first example of cyberwarfare that may disrupt the delivery of vital services, the 2007 Russian hack on Estonia's national infrastructure served as a warning to governments worldwide. Targeted cyberattacks are now a top priority for worldwide security as a result of this incident and subsequent government-funded hacking activities, corporate spying, and intellectual property theft.

6. EXPANDING DIGITAL ATTACK SURFACES

In contemporary online space, where the cloud infrastructure is widespread, remote working models have become popular, and a variety of third-party integrations are ubiquitous, the variety of potential points of entry into organizational systems has become significantly larger. A combination of these entry points is referred to as the attack surface. The knowledge and control of this surface is one of the primary steps to enhance the cybersecurity posture.

The digital ecosystems of organizations grow more complex as more organizations start embracing cloud services, mobile endpoints, and external applications. The result of such expansion is a direct increase in the attack surfaces, and visibility, monitoring, and control become critical.

Definition of Attack Surface

An attack surface is what can be described as any point in a digital environment that can be used by an unauthorized party, either an external attacker or an insider, to attack systems, steal data, or otherwise subvert the operation of the systems. They are exposed infrastructure, unsecured terminals, third-party connections and human connections.

An attack surface that is larger and more complex increases the chances of vulnerability, hence increasing the overall cyber risk associated with an organization.

Major Types of Attack Surface

There are three general types of attack surfaces.

1. **External attack surface**

   The external attack surface consists of anything accessible over the public internet, which is an excellent target for threat actors to scan and identify the gaps. Common components include:

   ◈ Web applications, domains, and subdomains

   ◈ Internet-facing APIs or databases

   ◈ Cloud infrastructure with exposed IPs or misconfigured buckets

   ◈ Third-party vendor connections with external access

2. **Internal attack surface**

   Although much attention is paid to external surfaces, the internal ones can also be very dangerous, particularly when an attacker manages to gain a foothold indoors. This category covers:

   ◈ Workstations, laptops, and mobile devices used by employees

- Internal servers, legacy applications, and databases
- Dev/test environments and staging systems
- Internal-only tools that lack strong authentication or encryption

3. **Social engineering attack surface**
   - Not every attack surface is technical. Humans are equally easy (or even more so) to exploit as software, and that exploitation is sometimes referred to as social engineering.
   - Indeed, shadow IT contributes significantly to increased risk. It is predicted that by 2027, 75 percent of workers will be using technology without the view of IT, which increases the human attack surface to control than ever. Examples here include:
   - Employee emails or helpdesk interactions
   - Public social media profiles used for impersonation
   - Phishing and pretexting targeting customer service reps
   - Contractors or third-party staff with elevated access

Importance of Understanding the Attack Surface

All the exposed or unsecured assets become entry points to the attackers. The more such assets one has, the higher the complexity of securing the assets. It is necessary to gain insights into the attack surface as it:

- Provides visibility into all potential vulnerabilities
- Enables prioritization of security efforts based on risk
- Supports security models such as Zero Trust
- Enhances threat detection and incident response capabilities

In essence, effective cybersecurity depends on a comprehensive understanding of all existing assets and exposures.

Evolution of the Attack Surface

Organizations do not remain the same so do their attack surfaces. That growth is due to the increased use of SaaS, cloud services, IoT, and mobile workforces. Each addition of a connection, dependency, or service brings a risk, which tends to happen in unexpected locations of security teams. As an example, new exposures may arise when:

- Spinning up a test server and forgetting to tear it down.
- Deploying a new app with default settings.
- Integrating with a third-party vendor that has weak security.
- Employee laptops accessing corporate systems from unsecured Wi-Fi.

Managing and Reducing the Attack Surface

Given the continuous expansion of attack surfaces, organizations must adopt a proactive and structured approach to security. The actual organization includes the following steps:

- **Asset Discovery.** Map every internet-accessible asset and every internal system or tool, including cloud services, containers, mobile endpoints, and third-party connections.
- **Risk Assessment.** Evaluate each exposure based on sensitivity, accessibility, and business criticality.
- **Risk Mitigation.** Apply practical controls: patching, disabling unused services, enforcing access policies, etc.
- **Continuous monitoring.** Use automation to detect changes in real time, especially in cloud and DevOps environments.

Real-World Examples of Attack Surface Exposure

Unmanaged or poorly monitored attack surfaces can lead to significant security incidents. Examples include:

- A development server was left active after deployment, exposing sensitive data

- An unsecured API is leaking customer information
- A third-party application integrated without proper authentication controls
- Remote devices accessing corporate systems through unsecured networks
- Public repositories containing exposed credentials or access tokens

Recent cybersecurity updates report on a major increase in vulnerability disclosures and the frequency of attacks, which point to increasing risks posed by unsecured attack surfaces.

7. INDUSTRY IMPLICATIONS OF CYBER RISK

The cyber risk has emerged as a major concern in all industries, considering the fact that increasingly more organizations are relying on interconnected digital systems. Cyberattacks are not isolated incidents as they can lead to a universal assault on different industries, economies, infrastructure, and social services.

The most striking one is the WannaCry ransomware attack (2017), which in a few hours has affected over 150 countries and has affected hospitals, banks, transportation systems, and businesses at the same time. Healthcare was also affected in that healthcare services were interrupted, surgeries cancelled and organizations were taken down. It was estimated that the overall economic impact was in the billions of dollars, and this shows that cyber incidents can have an impact on a whole industry, not just one organization.

Economic and Systemic Impact

There are financial losses that can be caused by cyber incidents not only to individual organizations but also to the economy as a whole. There are losses that occur due to loss in operational time, data breaches, recovery, and loss of business.

More to the point, cyber risk has systemic economic effects, in which the effect of disruption in one sector diffuses out to other sectors. The current business landscape of the industries is very much interconnected, such that when a business fails in one aspect, the repercussions may spread through its supply chains and the other supporting services.

To illustrate this, telecommunication failure may affect financial transactions, retail business and even medical services. Cyber incidents have more extensive economic implications when there are such interdependencies.

Interconnected Industry Risks

The digital economy today depends on common technologies in the form of operating systems, cloud platforms and software services. This will give rise to what is commonly known as a monoculture, where most organizations are relying on the same technological infrastructure.

On the one hand, this enhances efficiency, but on the other, it is more vulnerable. One exploited vulnerability in popular systems can affect thousands or even millions of users at the same time. The WannaCry virus proved that a simple vulnerability can cause a disruption around the world.

Also, the increased use of technologies like artificial intelligence (AI), Internet of Things (IoT), and 5G connectivity further increases interdependencies, scaling and unpredictability of cyber risks.

Sector-Wide Disruptions

Depending on the target and the intensity of the attack, cyberattacks can cause a disruption in the whole industry sector. Some such disruptions are:

- Attacks in the healthcare sector, in which hospitals are not able to access patient records and vital systems.
- Thousands of businesses were dependent on cloud service providers when the providers failed.
- Telecommunication outages, which affect connectivity and online services.

- Affecting manufacturing, energy and transportation, industrial control system attacks.
- Such cases demonstrate that cyber risk is not specific to individual companies, but can affect whole industries and critical infrastructure.

Strategic and Policy Implications

- The increasing magnitude of cyber risk has enormous impacts on the insurers, organizations and policymakers.
- Insurers need to evaluate systemic cyber risks and determine a coverage model that considers losses that are interconnected.
- Companies are forced to find essential dependencies, invest in resilience and be ready to face disruptions on a massive scale.
- To improve the level of cybersecurity, policymakers must devise a regulatory framework and encourage collaboration across industries.
- Cyber risk is increasingly turning into a systemic economic and national security problem, rather than a technical problem.

MULTIPLE CHOICE QUESTIONS (MCQS)

1. **What is cyber risk?**

   A. Risk of hardware failure

   B. Risk of financial loss due to inflation

   C. Risk associated with digital systems and data breaches

   D. Risk of natural disasters

2. **Which factor has most contributed to cyber risk at scale?**

   A. Decrease in internet usage

   B. Growth of interconnected digital systems

   C. Reduction in data storage

   D. Decline in mobile devices

3. **Early cyber threats were mainly characterized by:**
   - A. State-sponsored espionage
   - B. Simple viruses and worms
   - C. AI-based attacks
   - D. Cryptocurrency fraud
4. **What distinguishes modern cyber threats from early ones?**
   - A. Less complexity
   - B. Reduced financial impact
   - C. Highly organized and targeted attacks
   - D. Limited global reach
5. **Cyber incidents can impact economies by:**
   - A. Increasing employment only
   - B. Disrupting financial systems and businesses
   - C. Reducing internet access permanently
   - D. Eliminating trade barriers
6. **What is cyber warfare?**
   - A. Physical conflict using weapons
   - B. Use of digital attacks by nations to damage another country
   - C. Trade war between countries
   - D. Legal disputes over technology
7. **State-sponsored cyber-attacks are typically aimed at:**
   - A. Personal entertainment
   - B. National security and strategic advantage
   - C. Reducing internet costs
   - D. Social media engagement

8. **What is meant by an expanding digital attack surface?**
   A. Decrease in digital devices
   B. Reduction in vulnerabilities
   C. Increase in connected devices and entry points for attacks
   D. Limiting access to networks
9. **Which of the following increases cyber risk exposure?**
   A. Offline systems only
   B. Use of strong encryption
   C. Adoption of cloud computing and IoT
   D. Regular software updates
10. **Why is understanding cyber risk important in the digital age?**
   A. To eliminate all cyber threats
   B. To ignore technological advancements
   C. To manage and mitigate potential damages
   D. To reduce internet usage

Answers

1	2	3	4	5	6	7	8	9	10
C	B	B	C	B	B	B	C	C	C

Chapter 2

NATIONAL CYBERSECURITY FRAMEWORKS AND POLICY ARCHITECTURE

8. OVERVIEW

Today, nations all over the world have adapted to cybersecurity as one of the essential foundations of national security, economic stability, and online governance, as cyber threats continue to change and revolutionize in size, scope, and impact. The reliance on the digital infrastructure, including financial and healthcare systems, and access to important utilities and government buildings, has resulted in the necessity of the creation of well-structured and robust cybersecurity policies by states (Ganguli & Contributors, 2024).

National cybersecurity systems offer an identification approach to managing and controlling cyber threats and restraining them nationally. These frameworks bring in the standards, guidelines, and best practices that may be adopted by governments, organizations, and critical sectors in enhancing their cybersecurity posture. They also make sure that there is uniformity in the manner of risk evaluation, management, and communication across industries.

This is no more parallel than policy architecture, that is, the larger ecosystem of laws, regulations, governance models and institutional mechanisms that enable cybersecurity. This will involve the data protection policies, incident reporting policies, national policies on cybersecurity and the functions of the governing bodies and the administration commissions. An integrated approach is a dynamic and aligned endeavor in the countering of cyber threats.

In this chapter, the author speaks about the national cybersecurity structure and policy structure. It discusses some of the widely used models that have been embraced by the majority, such as the NIST Cybersecurity Framework and other global standards, with reference to their guides in risk management and resiliency. The other contribution of the governments in cybersecurity policies, improving collaboration between the people and privacy, and international collaboration, is also discussed in the chapter.

Besides, the chapter assesses the design and execution of different countries in their approach to cybersecurity as per the state of technology development, environment of risk, and regulations. It highlights the necessity of adaptable and multipurpose designs that can accommodate emerging technologies like cloud computing, artificial intelligence, and the Internet of Things.

The awareness of national cybersecurity frameworks and policy structure will allow organizations and policy makers to make their plans more aligned with the global standards, resilient to cyber-attacks, and to safely go digital in the ever-more digitalized global environment.

9. FOUNDATIONS OF NATIONAL CYBERSECURITY STRATEGIES

Cybersecurity is a very critical concern in the digital age that has been taken seriously by governments, organizations, and individuals. An effective and thorough National Cyber Security Strategy (NCSS) is necessary due to the quick growth of the digital ecosystem and the rise in cyber threats.

A National Cyber Security Strategy is a comprehensive plan designed to protect the nation's digital ecosystem by securing vital information infrastructure, enhancing data security and cyber resilience, forming partnerships with stakeholders, and responding to newly emerging cyber threats to provide both economic stability and national security.

Objectives of National Cybersecurity Strategies

Most national strategies on cybersecurity are usually based on a set of key objectives that jointly guarantee the safety, resiliency, and robustness of the online environment of a country:

- **Strengthening Cyber Defenses:** A key goal of any national cybersecurity strategy is to establish powerful mechanisms to defend against cyberattacks upon critical information infrastructure. This involves protecting networks, systems and digital assets against unauthorized access, malware, ransomware and other cyberattacks. Another concern of governments is to increase the threat detection mechanisms and develop effective defensive architectures to minimize vulnerabilities.
- **Promoting Data Protection:** This is another important goal that should be promoted to ensure that data is confidential, intact, and available. National strategies focus on the development of structures and policies that ensure that critical information is not compromised, abused, or revealed to unauthorized personnel. It entails the adoption of laws, encryption standards and robust data management protocols in the government as well as the private world.
- **Increasing Cooperation:** Cybersecurity is a shared responsibility, and best practices are promoting cooperation between the government agencies, commercial groups, and international organizations. Working together improves the nation's overall resilience by sharing threat intelligence, best practices, and coordinated efforts to address cyber events.
- **Capacity Building:** The critical factor in the management of cyber risks is building up skilled human resources and institutional capacity. The national strategies revolve around educating the cybersecurity specialists, enhancing education

and awareness, and creation of the technical expertise to address the augmented requirement of cybersecurity specialists.

The necessity of a national strategy for cyber security

The growing use of electronic technologies and the rising speed of development of online services have put the issue of cybersecurity on the agenda of the country. The necessity to possess an organized and holistic plan is grounded on a number of key factors.

- **Rising Cyber Threats:** The digitization that has grown fast has raised a wide range of cyber threats which include phishing, ransomware, data breach and advanced persistent threats. With the sophistication and frequency of cyberattacks, nations have to ensure that they are proactive in the measures adopted, which would enable them to identify and mitigate them.
- **Growth of Digital Transactions:** The increasing use of digital platforms to make financial transactions, e-commerce, and offer its services to the population has increased the attack surface. These transactions are paramount in securing confidence in the digital systems and steadiness of the digital economy.
- **Protection of Critical Infrastructure:** Essential sectors of economic activity, such as energy, banking, healthcare and defense, are common to cyberattacks. Such shocks in these areas can severely affect national security and personal safety, and therefore, one of their main preferences in national cybersecurity policies is to secure them.
- **Geopolitical Risks:** The cyber war has been one of the significant arms of the state and non-state actors. Cyber espionage, sabotage and politically motivated attacks, these represent an ever-increasing menace to nations, and this must be addressed at the national level through synchronized and strategic action.

- **Emerging Technologies:** The digital ecosystems are being changed by the technologies of 5G, Internet of Things (IoT), and Artificial Intelligence and create new threats. Under the national cybersecurity strategies, the emerging challenges should be addressed by bringing up futuristic security measures.

The necessity of a national cybersecurity strategy and its components

The National Cyber Security Strategy provides the essential elements to protect India's digital environment. It emphasizes effective security, fortifying institutional frameworks and fostering collaboration on creative strategies that make it resilient to changing cyberthreats.

1. **Security Strategies:** The security strategies focus on providing protection to critical assets and infrastructure by focusing on issues such as digitization, supply chain security, protection of critical information infrastructure, and emerging technologies. They guarantee a robust state, economic development and the security of citizens against changing cybersecurity threats.
2. **Strengthening Strategies:** It is essential to strengthen strategies in cybersecurity so that the expanding digital economy in India can be secured. Some of the key interventions are strengthening institutional structures, budgetary allocations, skills building, audit structures, and putting in place strong crisis management mechanisms so as to curtail the emerging cyber risks.
3. **Synergizing Strategies:** Some of the strategies that should be synergized to improve the situation in India with the cybersecurity issue include the improvement of the internet infrastructure, the creation of technical standards, promotion of cybersecurity under the brand India, the advancement of cyber diplomacy and strengthening cybercrime investigations by means of innovation and strategic investments.

Challenges of the National Cybersecurity Strategy

The National Cyber Security Strategy faces a number of obstacles, including a lack of qualified personnel, fragmented organizational structures, evolving cyber threats, inadequate funding, and public ignorance. When it comes to the mechanisms of successful cyber resilience, all of these needs should be addressed carefully.

- **Absence of Skilled Workforce:** India also lacks skilled cybersecurity professionals, which has exposed the critical infrastructure to sophisticated attacks. This gap must be filled with particular focus on the capacity building and special training programs.
- **Disjointed Cybersecurity Framework:** The absence of a single and integrated cybersecurity framework in India complicates the identification and response to a threat. The government agencies, the private sectors and the stakeholders involved need to be coordinated to have a good defense mechanism.
- **Shifting Character of Threats:** Cybersecurity threats presented through new technologies are more complicated as a result of quantum computing, artificial intelligence, and the internet of things. These emerging dynamic technologies demand that security frameworks be constantly updated and that active measures be taken to fix the loopholes.
- **Budget Constraints:** Practical cybersecurity initiatives are expensive in terms of financial investments. The lack of funds usually does not allow implementing new technologies, developing infrastructure, and the finding of professionals to work on cybersecurity projects.
- **Limited Public Awareness:** Although there are initiatives such as digital literacy campaigns, some of the citizens are not aware of simple online hygiene practices. Such a loophole further exposes phishing, fraud and data breaches and requires large-scale sensitization efforts.

10. REGULATORY AND COMPLIANCE ECOSYSTEMS

Regulatory compliance can be defined as the absolute adherence of an organization to comply with the applicable laws, rules, and standards of the industry, as well as the ethical conduct. Through adopting the aspect of regulatory compliance, organizations are in a position to ensure that their operations are carried out in such a way that they fit into the set rules and guidelines. This ethical commitment acts as a guide that helps organizations to become ethical, to comply with the law, to survive in business, and to maintain the trust of the stakeholders.

A legal checklist is just one aspect of regulatory compliance. It addresses compliance control in many different areas, including financial reporting, data privacy, environmental protection, and health and safety. Each of these domains has its own set of rules and guidelines, and organizations must be well-versed in the intricate regulatory landscape in which they operate. Managing this complex environment is an active process that is characterized by ongoing regulatory change control, thorough risk analysis, and the implementation of efficient internal rules.

It is difficult to overstate the significance of regulatory compliance. By preventing businesses from facing hefty fines, reputational harm, and even criminal penalties, it serves as a protective measure against legal ramifications. It plays a crucial part in safeguarding sensitive data, shielding businesses and their stakeholders from the dangers of cyber-attacks and data breaches. This is accomplished by making sure businesses adhere to regulations, which demonstrates their commitment to moral business conduct and fosters confidence among clients, investors, and other significant stakeholders.

Importance of Regulatory Compliance

Since compliance is not a cost, it is a way to promote integrity, increase trust, and ensure that an organization's reputation is maintained.

In addition to helping firms reduce risks, adhering to industry rules and standards also gives them a reputation for reliability, making them the cornerstones of credibility in a cutthroat commercial environment. Customers and other stakeholders view them as trustworthy partners because of their uncompromising ethical and transparent business practices.

Compliance is more than simply being a risk-averse compliance officer; it also protects an organization's most important asset, its data. In a time when data breaches and privacy issues are becoming more common, putting sensible data protection principles into practice will enable safeguarding consumer privacy, which will increase trust and provide businesses a competitive edge in a market that prioritizes privacy.

Compliance is an internal, rather than an external, guiding tool that gives employees a deep sense of their ethical and legal obligations. The provided awareness reduces the possibility of non-compliance and shows a supportive workplace culture that encourages moral behavior.

Regulation compliance is, in essence, one of the pillars of long-term corporate success rather than a box to be checked. Additionally, it is a preventative approach that reduces financial and legal risks, enhances brand perception, protects sensitive customer data, and fosters an ethical culture. Organizations that follow the rules will eventually experience long-term success, gain the trust of their customers, and gain a competitive edge that will help them advance in the constantly shifting regulatory environment.

How can businesses comply with regulations

A crucial goal that organizations should pursue is regulatory compliance. Several practical steps might be taken to ensure that businesses are risk-averse and compliance with regulations:

The first step is to implement a compliance management system. This system must have defined policies, procedures, and internal controls, like the specific compliance regulations that are applicable to the organization. To be in touch with the regulatory changes, it is necessary to monitor and update the compliance management system on a regular basis.

Secondly, the identification of possible gaps and vulnerabilities in compliance should be carried out through risk assessment and audit.

These tests must be carried out on a regular basis and cover every aspect of regulatory compliance, including financial reporting, data privacy, environmental restrictions, and other occupational health and safety requirements.

Thirdly, companies have to concentrate on educating and educating staff members. To maintain compliance throughout, personnel must receive training on their roles and responsibilities in adhering to regulatory obligations. A compliance culture can be instilled in the organization through regular training opportunities and seminars.

Fourth, the establishment and implementation of explicit rules and processes should be the most crucial aspect of financial compliance. These rules should be well-developed and distributed to every employee, outlining the organization's expectations for compliance. To ensure that these policies continue to be successful, they must be regularly updated and reviewed.

Lastly, automation and technology may greatly ease compliance. Customized software applications for data management, risk assessment, and reporting can help with regulatory compliance, lower the quantity of manual compliance tasks, and improve overall productivity.

Organizations may be able to navigate the regulatory environment, reduce compliance risks, and gain a competitive edge in the current market climate by putting these measures in place and establishing a culture of compliance.

Examples of Regulatory Compliance

We can explore some of the most prominent frameworks that impact industries in a meaningful way to get a better understanding of aspects of regulatory compliance:

The Sarbanes-Oxley Act (SOX) is one of the cornerstones of US corporate governance and financial reporting. In an effort to improve accountability and openness in financial reporting, SOX was implemented in 2002 in the wake of many corporate scandals. High standards of corporate governance, financial disclosure, and internal controls are necessary to provide investor protection and market trust.

The General Data Protection Regulation (GDPR) of the European Union, which went into effect in 2018, is among the most recent advancements in the field of data privacy. People now have more control over their personal data because to GDPR, which mandates that businesses have robust data protection procedures. Heavy fines and a reputational disaster might result from noncompliance with GDPR.

The security and privacy of any patient's health information in the healthcare sector are safeguarded under the Health Insurance Portability and Accountability Act (HIPAA). HIPAA provides patient information confidentiality and fosters patient confidence in the healthcare system by establishing comprehensive regulations for the protection, storage, and transfer of protected health information.

Lastly, a crucial step in protecting private cardholder data is the Paycard Industry Data Security Standard (PCI DSS). PCI DSS offers fundamental security procedures that aid in preventing fraud and data breaches, which are pertinent to organizations that handle, store, or transfer credit card-related data. To maintain the trust of card networks and clients, PCI DSS compliance is essential.

Common Regulatory Compliance Challenges

The regulatory compliance will be required to be done in an active and holistic fashion. It involves the investment in specialized compliance professionals, the presence of extensive risk assessment, the presence of excellent technology solutions, and the presence of an intensive employee training program. These investments are not costs alone, and they are defenses which organisations will require against the potential risks and legal pitfalls.

Failure to comply, on the other hand, can be crushing in other than money terms. It can ruin the image of an organization, ruin consumer loyalty, and disrupt business operations. The issue of regulatory compliance is not an option, and a requirement of sustainable development in the business setting, where trust is the key to winning.

To negotiate the problems of regulatory compliance successfully, organizations must be proactive. The introduction of effective compliance management systems and the creation of a compliance culture at all levels are also critical measures. This is not only to ensure that there is legal compliance, but also due to a responsibility to their operations to be ethical and responsibility-oriented. Anticipating compliance issues is better, as organizations will achieve a competitive advantage and foster trust among stakeholders, putting the organizations in a position that is likely to achieve success in the long term.

Regulatory compliance is actually not a liability, but it is a competitive edge. Compliance as the core value of an organization brings the organization to the top of the industry, making it a source of trust and confidence to the customers, partners and investors. It is a journey towards sustainable success, which guarantees them leadership in the business space. Compliance is therefore a strategy that helps an organization to not only protect itself against risks but also create a competitive advantage and survive in the dynamic business environment.

11. PUBLIC-PRIVATE PARTNERSHIPS IN CYBER DEFENSE

In the modern digitalized society where cyberspace is a key location in terms of the commercial world as well as national security, cybersecurity has grown beyond merely a technical issue to become a strategic necessity. It is not confined to information technology systems anymore but has become an element of the national security systems.

The contemporary governments are confronted with a swiftly changing threat environment, including transnational cybercriminal networks and state-sponsored entities. Such attackers tend to attack digital infrastructure, which is mostly owned and governed by the private sector, which holds a major share of the key assets, including energy grids, financial machinery, and telecommunication networks.

This poses a basic issue of operation: even though governments are in charge of national security, the digital infrastructure is a matter of control by private organizations to a large extent. This renders the traditional top-down-based solutions to cybersecurity insufficient. A paradigm of collaborative and interdependent governance is needed to attain successful cyber defense, whereby the government and the private sectors can work together in terms of preventing, detecting, responding to, and recovering from threats.

The partnerships between the government and companies (PPP) provide such a framework. Governments and nongovernmental organizations are structured through these alliances to share information about the critical intelligence concerning the threats in real time, coordinate their responses to such events, and develop a mutual understanding of the risks and also invest in cybersecurity capabilities. PPPs can contribute to the national cyber resilience by bringing together the power of the government and the innovation and operation capabilities of the corporate sector.

However, PPPs have been adopted in an unequal manner, even with their enhanced importance. Issues such as uncertainty in the law, lack of trust, misalignment of incentives and lack of sufficient standardization structure are still significant barriers to their performance. More formal, scaled and institutionalized collaborations between the state and business have become necessary as cyber threats become more sophisticated and more involved.

Importance of Public-Private Partnerships in Cyber Défense

The nature of the cyber threat has changed and thus the traditional means of defense is not very effective. Cybersecurity Public-Private Partnerships allow a highly effective defense strategy by integrating government agencies with companies so as to collectively share the intelligence as well as to distribute resources and to plan. The merger of the two industries can yield:

- **Improved Threat Intelligence:** Organizations can exchange real-time information and threat data, which enables faster response times.
- **Optimized Resource Allocation:** It is possible to resource-pool to allocate resources and efforts in a more strategic manner, leading to an improved security framework overall.

- **Stronger Compliance and Ethics Standards:** Agreement on the ethical practice will help to reduce risks connected with data mishandling and make more stakeholders trust the company.

Best Practices for Successful Public-Private Partnerships in Cyber Defense

To maximize the effectiveness of public-private partnerships in cybersecurity, organizations should consider the following best practices:

1. **Establish Clear Objectives:** Effective collaborations are based on having clear and congruent goals. Both the stakeholders in the two sectors should establish what they look to accomplish by working together, be it enhancing the intelligence of threats, enhancing compliance or improving the overall security.
2. **Promote Open Communication:** Communication may be very effective in influencing the success of PPPs. Constant changes, feedback and sharing of information promote transparency and trust, thereby establishing an enabling environment to work together.
3. **Implement Joint Training Programs:** Training programs involving the staff of the public and the private sector will boost skills and centralize the response measures. The joint training also ensures the reinforcement of knowledge as well as the development of camaraderie that enhances the efficiency of the joint operations.
4. **Foster a Culture of Compliance:** The culture of compliance should be the top priority of HR in organizations at all levels. When stakeholders realize that ethical conduct and compliance are the collective roles, they will be in a position to collaborate to achieve common objectives.
5. **Evaluate and Adapt Strategies:** The ever-changing cyber threat environment also requires constant review of strategies to make sure organizations can cope. Routine evaluations

enable partners to re-allocate resources and plans on the premise of real-time information and mutual knowledge.

Examples of Public–Private Partnerships in Cyber Defense

Cases in the real world indicate the success of the collaboration between the government and industry regarding cybersecurity:

- **Information Sharing and Analysis Centers (ISACs):** Industry-specific mechanisms like financial and energy ISACs allow organizations to exchange threat information and organize response activities to cyber-attacks.
- **Cybersecurity and Infrastructure Security Agency (CISA) - Private Sector Collaboration:** CISA is closely involved in collaboration with the private organizations in the United States to exchange threat intelligence, joint exercises, and the enhancement of critical infrastructure protection.
- **Global Response to Ransomware Attacks:** In case of such massive ransomware attacks, governments and various cybersecurity agencies cooperate to monitor attacks, exchange signatures of intrusion, and prevent extensive losses.

These illustrations show that the synergistic collaboration between the government and the business community can contribute to cybersecurity resilience on the national and international levels.

12. INTERNATIONAL CYBER NORMS AND COOPERATION

This cyberspace has gained a critical sector of economic operation, the rule and the national security in the modern digital world. The cyber threats are not limited to the borders of a certain country as digital systems are still becoming interconnected among countries. The aspect of cybersecurity has become an international challenge because the point of attack may be situated in a specific region and affect multiple nations at the same time.

In this respect, international cyber norms have become a significant tool for regulating the operations of the state in cyberspace.

These standards are generic norms of how responsible behaviour is expected to be, and the orientation here is to minimize conflicts, ensure the protection of the critical infrastructure, and the provision of an unwavering global digital environment. Such norms are not necessarily binding, but they play a significant role in policies and make sure that trust exists between the nations.

At the same time, international cooperation is one of the main components of an effective response to cyber threats. The global cyberspace is something that cannot be totally visualized or controlled by a single country. Cooperation aids the nations to share intelligence on threats, organize the actions and agree on the joint strategies to overcome the threats and prevent escalation.

However, the degree of effective cooperation is not simple due to the differences in national interests, legal frameworks, and technical opportunities. Regardless of such challenges, additional engagement in the international collaboration and the development of internationally accepted standards is necessary to achieve a stable cyberspace.

Concept of International Cyber Norms

Cybernorms are unofficial guidelines and precepts that promote appropriate state behavior in the virtual world.

By providing guidelines that nations and other interested parties might adopt in an effort to lessen cyber dangers and prevent cyber war, they are intended to enhance international security and stability.

These standards are intended to promote collaboration, openness, and trust between nations and other players in the digital sphere, even if they are not legally obligatory. Effective communication, teamwork in technical controls, and attempting to hold the offenders accountable should all be part of the use of cybernorms.

The key cyber norms include:

1. **Non-use of ICTs for Internationally Wrongful Acts:** States shall not engage in or knowingly encourage ICT activity that purposefully destroys vital infrastructure or otherwise hinders its use and functioning to deliver services to the general public.

2. **Protection of Critical Infrastructure:** States should take the necessary precautions to guard against ICT threats to their critical infrastructure.
3. **Incident Response Cooperation:** States shall react appropriately when another State's vital infrastructure is the target of harmful ICT activities.
4. **Respect for Human Rights:** When using ICTs, states should uphold fundamental freedoms and human rights.
5. **Non-interference in Internal Affairs:** States shall refrain from engaging in or knowingly endorsing ICT activities that purposefully harm or hinder the usage and functioning of vital infrastructure in order to exert political pressure or destabilize another state.
6. **Non-exploit of Proxies:** States shall refrain from utilizing proxies to exploit ICTs to commit crimes against international law.
7. **Responsible Reporting of Vulnerabilities:** In order to reduce and perhaps eliminate possible risks to ICTs and ICT-dependent infrastructure, states should promote responsible reporting of ICT vulnerabilities and exchange related information on available remedies to remedy such vulnerabilities.
8. **Respect for International Law:** States must acknowledge the relevance and need of international law, particularly the UN Charter, in preserving peace and stability and fostering an ICT environment that is open, safe, stable, accessible, and peaceful.
9. **Cooperation for Stability and Security:** States should work together to create and implement policies that promote stability and security in the use of ICTs and to stop detrimental or potentially dangerous ICT activities.
10. **Capacity Building:** States should think about the best ways to work together to help developing nations create and implement strategies to safeguard their vital infrastructures and address ICT security.

Need for Global Cyber Cooperation

One of the biggest contemporary threats to international security is information and communications technology (ICT). According to threat assessments, a state or terrorist organization using ICTs as a weapon to destroy vital infrastructure or military logistical networks might be the cause of the next significant global catastrophe. The use of ICTs by governments has expanded due to the rise of asymmetric warfare, or battles between nations or organizations with different military capabilities. This calls for the creation of an international code of cyber behavior.

To combat threats like cybercrime, cyberattacks on vital infrastructure, electronic espionage, mass data interception, and offensive operations meant to project power through the use of force in and through cyberspace, governments must work together immediately. International activity should be reorganized to take into account the likelihood that emerging cyberthreats may cause enormous economic and social harm.

One of the most common misconceptions is that the biggest cyberthreats that call for immediate international cooperation are massive, state-funded attacks that destroy vital infrastructure facilities like power plants or electrical systems, causing enormous damage and fatalities. In actuality, cyber dangers are more varied and complex, and they can impact specific businesses in addition to endangering the technical security of the online environment. Due to the nearly total digitalization of business models, the world economy is vulnerable to cyberattacks by criminal groups and other nonstate actors in addition to nations.

The increasing computerization of the global economy has made nations more vulnerable to cyberattacks and more prone to one another. These dangers affect not just state actors but also non-state actors like cybercriminal groups. They cannot effectively address these dangers on their own, which is why strong international cooperation, information sharing, and reaction action coordination are crucial.

Key Principles of Responsible State Behavior

Cyber norms are rules and principles in cyberspace, which are voluntary and encourage responsible behaviour among states. They are created to improve international security and stability by offering a guideline that states and other interested parties can use in an attempt to reduce cyber threats and avert cyber conflict.

The 11 voluntary and non-binding cyber norms were initially created in 2015 and were agreed upon in the United Nations Groups of Governmental Experts (GGE) and subsequently reaffirmed by all UN Member States in the Open-Ended Working Group (OEWG) processes.

These norms are part of the UN system of responsible state behaviour which also requires compliance with international law, guarding crucial infrastructure, avoiding mafios activities like cyber espionage and electoral interference and due diligence so that non-state actors would not use a territory or ICT infrastructure of a state to perpetrate wrong acts.

These norms are not binding, but they have the purpose of developing cooperation, transparency, and trust between states and other players in the digital space. Nonetheless, their application continues to be a challenge, and it takes a long-lasting discussion, technical collaboration, and mechanisms to deal with infractions. Meanwhile, there is still a divergence between the states, with some believing that the current structure is adequate as long as it is implemented to the fullest extent, and others believe that more norms should be created, including the introduction of new binding requirements to make that regime more accountable.

In their setup of a new single-track permanent mechanism named the Global Mechanism on developments in the field of ICTs in the context of international security and advancing responsible State behaviour in the use of ICTs, the Final Report of the OEWG 2021-2025 establishes further discussion of five pillars of the framework, such as implementation of the agreed cyber norms.

Simultaneously, various multistakeholder programs are dealing with how to practically implement the norms, and the non-state actors involved include the private sector, academia, the technical community, and civil society. The Geneva Dialogue on Responsible Behaviour in Cyberspace is one such initiative, and the results and observations of the same are reflected in the Geneva Manual, which offers insights and views on how the norms can be implemented.

Role of International Organizations and Stakeholders

There are many different potential parties involved in the creation of cybersecurity standards. There are many different players involved, each with their own motivations, skill levels, cultures, and ideals. Governments must work with the ICT sector, academia, and civil society. Because they worry about how it would affect their options for national security, governments may steer clear of developing cybersecurity standards that restrict conflict. This viewpoint is misguided since it undermines the trust of businesses, citizens, and other governments in addition to ignoring the government's other functions as an ICT user and guardian. In the long term, this lack of trust would weaken the state's ability to defend itself, its inhabitants, and its national interests by impeding economic development, technological innovation, and civil society involvement.

The duties and expectations of the government, business, and general public with regard to public safety and national security are evolving rapidly as the Information Age progresses. Data is growing exponentially thanks to ICT advancements, which are also generating capabilities that were previously only available to governments with the financial means to spend money on R&D without seeing results right away. All parties, not just governments, need to be ready to cope with differences, adjust to changes, and continuously learn in this complicated environment.

The requirement for many partners in cybersecurity operations is not a philosophy but rather a practical reality. The creation of cybersecurity standards cannot be a specialized foreign policy concern that only diplomats can handle. In an Internet-dependent world, cybersecurity standards are essential for all users, governments, the commercial sector, non-governmental organizations (NGOs), and individuals—all of which contribute to the peace, security, and ongoing innovation of a globally interconnected society. While accepting that not all stakeholders may be equal participants in every endeavor due to varying levels of competence, these stakeholders can and should offer their skills to the norm formation process. The commercial sector, academia, and civil society will be able to contribute significantly to the development of soft norms that eventually become customary international law. However, countries should continue to have the authority to enact laws and approve prospective treaties, subject to national political procedures.

Challenges in International Cyber Cooperation

Despite the growing importance of international collaboration in cybersecurity, several challenges continue to hinder effective cooperation among nations.

- **Rapid Technological Advancements:** The pace of technological change in the cybersecurity landscape is incredibly rapid. As a result, research findings may become outdated quickly, and emerging threats or technologies might not be adequately addressed in the study.
- **Attribution Challenges:** Identifying cyber-attacks to a given actor is one of the longstanding problems in the cybersecurity arena. Cyber threat actors use the anonymity and obfuscation tools that make it challenging to attribute attacks with certainty, which affects the reliability of the analysis of state-sponsored activities.
- **Lack of Transparency:** There is a certain level of secrecy in the way nation-states deal with their cybersecurity policies and capabilities. A lack of transparency may cause difficulties in the full perception of the actions taken by states in combating cyber threats, so the analysis may be incomplete or biased.
- **Differing National Perspectives:** States have diverse views concerning cyber security depending on their geopolitical background, cultural values and their past experiences. The process of establishing worldwide security standards together with international agreements will be hindered by these

inconsistencies, which lead to different interpretations of cybersecurity threats and their corresponding solutions.

- **Geopolitical Tensions:** International cooperation on cybersecurity protection will face difficulties because of existing geopolitical disputes and international power struggles between nations. Political factors and historical animosities, together with trust deficits, create obstacles that prevent countries from establishing collaborative mechanisms to handle cyber threats effectively.
- **Legal and Regulatory Challenges:** Countries establish separate legal frameworks, together with distinct cybersecurity laws, which create substantial differences between their legal systems. The existing legal traditions, together with distinct privacy practices and national security requirements, create obstacles that hinder the integration of these systems for international security cooperation.
- **Resource Disparities:** Nations have large differences in resources and capabilities to deal with cybersecurity challenges. The developing and economically disadvantaged nations might struggle to put strong barriers on cybersecurity and may widen the world's cyber inequality.
- **Unintended Consequences:** The reactions of the states to cyber threats can also have some unintended results, such as the worsening of tensions or the introduction of restrictions that have a negative influence on the freedoms of individuals. The prospective unintended consequences of the actions of the state are a complicated and difficult task to analyze.
- **Evolving Nature of Cyber Threats:** There is a continuous change in cyber threats and their enemies are changing the approaches and methods of attack. The threats that may arise are hard to predict and respond to, and the response of the states might be restricted by the dynamical character of the cybersecurity environment.

- **Ethical Considerations:** Ethical concerns are posed by the use of offensive cyber capabilities, such as the issue of proportionality, collateral damage, and the possible militarization of cyberspace. Ethical concerns may not be adequately addressed in state responses and international agreements.

13. RISK GOVERNANCE AND NATIONAL RESILIENCE MODELS

Cyber risks are one of the key issues that are of concern to governments, organizations, and societies in the dynamic digital world. The possibilities of the cyber threat have evolved tremendously as countries continue to base their economic activities, governance, and other vital services on digital infrastructure. The control of these risks will involve more than only technical controls but also established governance procedures that can direct the decision-making process, the formulation of policy and coordinated response plans at the national level.

Risk governance can be defined as the systems, policies and institutional facilities around which cyber risks are discovered, extended and controlled. It entails various parties such as the government agencies, the private sector organizations and regulatory bodies collaborating to ensure that risks are handled in an organized and open way. Good risk governance helps nations to concentrate on essential assets, distribute resources effectively and proactively react to new threats.

The very concept of national resilience is closely related to risk governance. National resilience is the capability of a nation to foresee, absorb, react and recuperate after disruptions, including cyber-attacks. Considering the area of cybersecurity, resiliency focuses not only on the ability to prevent attacks but also on the ability to continue functioning and swiftly recover following negative occurrences.

Contemporary perspectives of cybersecurity point to the necessity of incorporating governance, risk management, and resilience in one framework. This integration means that countries will be in a better position to cope with uncertainties, reduce the effects of cyber-attack and maintain professional stability in an environment that is increasingly linked.

Concept of Risk Governance

Risk governance is based on a broad understanding of risk as defined by the International Risk Governance Council (IRGC), which describes risk as "uncertainty about the consequences of an activity or event with respect to something that humans value." This aligns with ISO 31000:2018, where risk is defined as "the effect of uncertainty on objectives," and risk management refers to the coordinated activities used to direct and control an organization with regard to risk.

Risk is often associated with change and is accompanied by both opportunities and potential negative consequences. Effective risk governance aims to enable societies to benefit from change while minimizing adverse impacts. Understanding risk involves analyzing factors such as severity, probability, exposure, vulnerability, and overall consequences.

Governance can be defined as the activities, procedures, customs and mechanisms involved in exercising authority and making and acting on decisions. Risk governance uses these principles to identify, evaluate, manage and communicate risks in a systematically and open way.

Risk governance in the global and systemic risks context demands international coordination and incorporation of various stakeholders such as governments, industries, scientific institutions and civil society. Such a collaborative strategy guarantees a comprehensive approach to risks and the opportunity to consider different opinions during decision-making.

The IRGC framework also highlights several important considerations for successful risk governance. These are enhancing the contribution of scientific knowledge in the process of policymaking, providing people and institutions with awareness of risks and their impacts, and evaluating their abilities to mitigate risks and address unforeseen incidents. It also emphasizes the significance of assessing the secondary impacts, finding the balance between societal and economic value in risk acceptance, precautionary strategies where needed, and the necessity to find the balance between inclusivity in decision-making and the urgency to act.

National Cyber Resilience and Its Importance

The capacity to stop, endure and rebound from cybersecurity assaults is known as cyber resilience. It unites business continuity, information systems security and organizational resilience and concentrates on the capacity to keep on delivering the desired outcomes even following some difficult cyber incidents.

The contemporary cyber threats have emerged with new challenges, and the environment we have now is such that operational security measures are not enough. Firms and countries are confronted with high-tech enemies who employ high-tech strategies and mechanisms to bring havoc. Instead of using conventional automated attacks, there is an increase in the use of human weaknesses and weaknesses in the system by threat actors.

Cyber resilience underlines that something must be done to prevent it. It understands that cyber incidents are unavoidable and aims to sustain the operations in case of disruptions and prompt recovery following an attack. This change underscores the value of resilience as a strategy of continuity and reducing the effect of cyber events.

The increasing use of digital systems has necessitated cyber resilience to support vital services. Nationally, vital infrastructure like energy systems, financial systems, health services, transport systems and communication platforms rely on digitally integrated systems. Cyberattacks may lead to disruptions in one sector that will have a ripple effect on other sectors, including economic stability, population safety and national security.

The national cyber resilience thus involves a unified action incorporating various stakeholders such as the government agencies, other companies in the private sector and the operators of the critical infrastructure. The fact that a significant part of digital infrastructure is operated by non-governmental forces means that cooperation and the exchange of information are important elements of resilience on a national level.

The changing threat environment, such as ransomware attacks, phishing, and sophisticated cyber activities, shows why resilience is becoming more and more necessary. Threats are increasingly becoming more complex, and more capabilities are necessary to respond, recover and adapt to the evolving dangers.

Besides that, national strategies are essential in creating resilience as they combine risk assessment, incident response planning, and recovery plans into a single structure. The governments are expected to establish policies, resource allocation and capabilities that would make them strengthened surveillance, prompt reaction and long-term adaptation to cyber threats.

Cyber resilience assists in the ability to be capable of continuing to operate despite unfavorable conditions and to ensure that systems and services can restore to their normal operations and performance without creating excessive havoc. This makes it one of the predictors of stability, security and continuity in an environment that is increasingly becoming digital and connected.

Risk Assessment and Management Frameworks (e.g., NIST RMF)

By integrating security and privacy into the system development lifecycle (SDLC), the NIST Risk Management Framework (RMF) guarantees early risk identification and mitigation. Because it enables continuous tracking and risk assessments, it is a versatile tool for adapting to the ever-changing threat environment.

It was first developed by the National Institute of Standards and Technology to provide businesses with a standard structure for managing cybersecurity threats. The framework was first created to support U.S. federal agencies, but because it may assist in resolving security challenges, it has gained significant popularity in other industries.

Important Elements of the NIST Framework for Risk Management

The RMF has seven fundamental steps, which aim at taking organizations through a systematic risk management process:

- **Prepare:** This is the base level at which organizations are prepared in order to handle the security and privacy risks. It entails the determination of risk management roles, determining the risk tolerance level of the organization, and defining the boundaries of the systems.
- **Categorize:** Systems are classified using the levels of the impacts of confidentiality, integrity, and availability. This stage identifies the level of risk, as well as the required security measures.
- **Select:** The right security controls are chosen based on the NIST Special Publication 800-53, based on the categorization of the system. The controls should be consistent with the organizational policies and must resolve the identified risks.
- **Implement:** The controls are implemented in the system, and they should be designed into the architecture and the operational environment of the system.
- **Assess:** The evaluation of security controls is conducted to identify the effectiveness of controls. This is a test engagement where the performance of the controls is tested, validated and documented.
- **Authorize:** The senior reviewer evaluates the outcome of the assessment and makes a decision to approve the system to operate or not, taking into account the residual risks.
- **Monitor:** Constant monitoring guarantees continuous evaluation and countermeasures against risks, which secures the security posture of the system in the long run.

Benefits of the NIST Risk Management Framework

There are a number of benefits of the implementation of the NIST RMF in the organization:

- **Enhanced Security Posture:** The RMF assists organizations in being proactive in dealing with vulnerabilities and threats because risk management is applied throughout the system lifecycle.

- **Regulatory Compliance:** The RMF is consistent with a range of regulatory frameworks such as the Federal Information Security Modernization Act (FISMA) and the General Data Protection Regulation (GDPR), which assist organizations in complying with the regulatory requirements.
- **Improved Decision-Making:** The framework will offer an organized way of risk assessment so that the firm can make informed decisions by having a clear picture of the risks and their possible effects.
- **Resource Optimization:** The RMF assists companies in allocating resources effectively by prioritizing risks and addressing the most important areas.
- **Adaptability:** RMF can be customized to meet the special requirements of various organizations of any size and industry.

Challenges of the NIST Risk Management Framework

Although the RMF has many advantages, its execution may be a challenging experience:

- **Resource Intensity:** The RMF is time-consuming, labor-intensive, and expensive to implement, especially for small organizations with limited resources.
- **Complexity:** It may be overwhelming to understand and implement the comprehensive guidelines in the RMF, particularly for organizations that are new to risk management.
- **Cultural Resistance:** There is the possibility of resistance to the transition to a risk-based approach by stakeholders who are used to the traditional security practices.
- **Continuous Monitoring:** A constant checking process consumes specific resources, and it takes the will to conduct frequent evaluation and review.
- **Tailoring the Framework:** It might be difficult to customize the RMF and make it meet the requirements of a particular

organization, so it may need a professional with proper planning.

Cybersecurity Governance Models and Standards (e.g., NIST CSF, ISO frameworks)

The US Department of Commerce's National Institute of Standards and Technology (NIST) is an entity that promotes innovation and expansion for businesses in the science and technology sector. The agency created the NIST CSF as a collection of principles to assist firms in developing and improving their security strategies in order to reduce cybersecurity risks. In contrast to certain standards, such as ISO 27001, NIST CSF is a set of guidelines that assist firms in developing a robust information security program rather than a means of demonstrating or certifying their security posture.

Despite being created by a government institution, the NIST CSF was intended to assist private sector firms in more accurately evaluating cybersecurity threats. Numerous organizations and several foreign governments utilize it.

The five roles of NIST

The framework's five main purposes are to identify, protect, detect, respond, and recover. Each of these features is necessary for your cybersecurity strategy in order to safeguard your resources and reduce the potential harm caused by a security breach, given the variety of methods hackers and cybercriminals might use to access your data.

1. **Identify:** The NIST CSF framework's first step is to clearly identify the assets and information that require protection. These covers establish roles and duties as well as hardware, software, datasets, and equipment.

2. **Protect:** Protecting assets to stop illegal access to systems and data is the main goal of the protect function. This entails putting in place security measures, including encryption, backups, updates, identity and access management, and training.

3. **Detect:** The detect function offers methods for spotting possible security flaws or breaches, allowing for prompt action to reduce harm. This entails keeping an eye out for suspicious behavior and illegal access to networks and systems.
4. **Reply:** Developing strategies and procedures to lessen the effects of a security breach and efficiently handle the situation is the main goal of the reply function.
5. **Recover:** Following a breach, retrieving data, fixing systems, and enhancing policies are all part of the recover function, which also involves preserving resilience.

NIST CSF's advantages

Adhering to the NIST CSF recommendations may enhance your company's cybersecurity posture in a number of ways, including:

- Professional advice on cybersecurity best practices, as opposed to creating a framework independently.
- The legitimacy of adhering to an industry norm.
- Adaptability to the requirements of your company.

ISO 27001 compliance

The International Organization of Standardization created a collection of security standards and procedures known as ISO 27001, which is an acronym for ISO/IEC 27001. The gold standard for international security best practices is the ISO security framework, which is utilized all over the world. Similar to NIST CSF, ISO 27001 outlines certain security measures, internal guidelines, and uniform procedures to assist companies in safeguarding their data against theft and abuse.

The three tenets of ISO 27001

The ISO 27001 standard is based on three fundamental ideas. These principles—confidentiality, information integrity, and data availability—are sometimes referred to as the CIA trinity.

1. **Confidentiality:** Only those who are authorized can access an organization's data according to the confidentiality principle. In order to prevent unauthorized users from accessing sensitive company data, firms must implement an information security management system (ISMS) in accordance with ISO 27001. Additionally, it mandates that information sent both inside and outside the company be encrypted to safeguard it while in transit.

2. **Integrity of information:** The information integrity principle guarantees that whatever data that a company has will remain accurate during storage and sharing. This implies that neither the entity in charge of the data nor malicious actors should delete, alter, or interfere with it. The information must remain exactly how it was produced or received.

3. **Data accessibility:** The availability of the organization's data is the last ISO 27001 principle. According to this idea, clients and staff must have access to the data they require for the intended business use. Only authorized users have this access.

The advantages of ISO 27001

The following advantages are offered to your company by an ISO 27001 certification:

- Provides you with an easy approach to use a worldwide standard to show your cybersecurity posture.
- By assisting you in implementing security best practices, it reduces the chance of an expensive cybersecurity compromise.
- Because of your solid security posture, it helps you draw in new customers and partners.

Multi-Stakeholder Collaboration in Risk Governance

Multi-stakeholder collaboration is defined as the inclusion of various groups and actors that are either affected by or interested in a system, policy or process. Such stakeholders are governments, the private sector organizations, academia, civil society and other interested parties who are affected or have an impact on risk governance decisions.

Stakeholder collaboration refers to the collaboration with these groups to communicate feedback, knowledge contribution, sharing of resources and working towards the shared goals. This partnership aids in the formation of more comprehensive and knowledgeable strategies of dealing with complex and changing risks in the context of risk governance.

The stakeholder cooperation may have various shapes, depending on the situation. Community collaboration entails the mobilization of the affected groups and the community in making decisions. Internal collaboration dwells on coordination within organizations such as leadership, groups and departments. Collaboration with organizations or groups entails the collaboration of various institutions like government agencies, firms, and non-governmental organizations in an attempt to accomplish common objectives.

Multi-stakeholder collaboration is significant because it improves the efficiency of risk governance. The stakeholders can also provide valuable sources of insights, skills, and resources by coming together to enhance the processes of making decisions. Teamwork allows the identification of possible risks in the initial stages and preconditions the creation of more efficient mitigation measures.

Teamwork also assists in the development of trust, transparency and accountability among the stakeholders. In cases of a multiplicity of actors in the processes of governance, decisions tend to be embraced and endorsed, which causes policies and strategies to be stronger in terms of implementation.

Moreover, the multi-stakeholder collaboration facilitates innovation through a combination of various ideas, knowledge, and strategies. It enables sharing of resources and capabilities among the stakeholders, enhancing efficiency and minimizing duplication of efforts. This is especially significant in cybersecurity, where risks are all related to each other, and they constantly develop across the fields and national borders.

Moreover, teamwork has made communication and understanding between stakeholders easier, as well as aligning goals and expectations. It also embraces sustainability because decisions made take into account long-term effects and the interests of various people.

Nevertheless, collaborating with multiple stakeholders may also be problematic. The variations in priorities, interests, and expertise levels of the stakeholders can give rise to conflicts or slowness of the decision-making. The integration of various actors proves to be a difficult process because it requires clear identification of their roles, their responsibilities and their methods of communication. The process of multi-stakeholder collaboration development serves as a vital element that enables effective risk governance despite existing obstacles. The system enables organizations to implement risk management strategies that work together with other systems to create stable and secure environments that protect their complex systems from disruptions.

14. INDUSTRY IMPLICATIONS OF CYBERSECURITY FRAMEWORKS

The cybersecurity systems have emerged as essential security instruments that can be applied by organizations in different fields in addressing cyber threats with a view of avoiding the loss of important assets in the new digital economy. As businesses depend on more and more connected systems and cloud platforms in addition to digital technologies, the need to possess systematic and standardized approaches to cybersecurity has grown exponentially. The cybersecurity frameworks provide an organization with a clear guideline and best practices to learn the vulnerability and improve the defenses and control the potential reaction to response to the arising threats.

This increased digitalization of modern businesses has entailed a broad range of new risks, and the management of cyber risks has become more difficult. Advanced attacks are susceptible in organizations and are directed towards technological and human. These risks can disrupt the functioning and disclose confidential data, not to mention numerous financial and reputation losses.

Another concern that has an impact on governance and accountability is the benefit of cybersecurity frameworks. Without a well-established framework, organizations may not be at ease because of the absence of accountability, visibility and the inconsistency of safety and proper management of risks. Frameworks help in delineating roles and responsibilities as well as policies that enable the leadership to make qualified decisions and be accountable in the process of controlling cybersecurity risks.

Also, along with cybersecurity frameworks, regulatory compliance and industry standards are present. In order to comply with the regulations, firms and organizations in other sectors, such as finance, health, and energy, must comply with various regulations linked to data protection and cybersecurity. Frameworks aid in compliance initiatives through standard processes and controls, which assist organizations in complying with the legal requirements and establishing trust with the stakeholders.

Effect on Security Posture and Risk Management

The process of locating, analyzing, assessing, resolving, and keeping an eye on cybersecurity risks to networked systems, data, and users is known as cyber risk management. This is intended to lower any possible risks and force companies to insure their businesses and assets.

Cybersecurity frameworks encourage firms to be risk-based rather than reactive because they should be proactive in their approach to risks and analyze them before they materialize through anticipation, assessment, and mitigation.

The initial process of this process is to identify assets, systems, data and processes and learn about their value to the organization. This is coupled with determining the possible threats and weaknesses that would affect these assets. Organizations will be in a good position to understand their risk exposure by examining the probability and the severity of these threats.

The major aspect of this approach is Risk prioritization, where organizations can concentrate on the most critical risks that may exert the most significant impact. This makes sure that resources are distributed in an efficient manner and the high-priority risks are considered within a good time.

The cybersecurity frameworks also assist organizations in choosing and applying proper controls that will reduce the identified risks. Such controls can be technical, policy-based, and training-based controls that are aimed at mitigating vulnerabilities and enhancing overall security.

Constant monitoring is also another thing that a good risk management should have. The cybersecurity models enable ongoing assessment of risks and controls that would enable the organizations to monitor the changes in the threat landscape and respond to them.

An important component of improving an organization's security posture is managing cyber threats. Identifying the risks involved and implementing preventative actions are the most effective ways for firms to lessen their exposure to cyber-attacks.

Every aspect of a company, including people, procedures, and even technology, is covered by an efficient cyber risk management strategy. This improves the overall security posture by strengthening all potentially vulnerable sectors in a holistic manner.

The key objective of cybersecurity risk management is to safeguard assets, property and business activities of a firm against cyber threats. Companies consequently endeavor to ensure the sustainability of their business activities without causing harm to sensitive information and ensuring the confidence of its customers through a well-designed, coordinated risk management and mitigation.

Regulatory and Compliance Implications

Cybersecurity compliance requires organizations to follow established security standards and regulations and legal requirements that protect their digital systems, networks and information assets. The process requires organizations to establish policies and procedures and controls that will enable them to achieve compliance with all applicable laws and regulations.

Cybersecurity compliance frameworks refer to organized policies, controls, and best practices that are aimed at assisting organizations to safeguard sensitive information and address regulatory demands. Such structures offer a uniform method of handling cybersecurity risks and, at the same time, maintaining compliance with legal and industry-related requirements.

The compliance frameworks are used to ensure that organizations adhere to legal requirements regarding cybersecurity practices by offering standard guidelines on data protection, access control, incident response, and incident monitoring. This helps organizations to ensure the compliance requirements are met in a systematic manner as well as improving their overall security status.

Organizations must adhere to certain regulations concerning cybersecurity and data protection in most industries. These standards make sure that sensitive information is treated with care and that organizations adhere to the same rigorous standards in the course of their businesses.

Violation of the rules of cybersecurity may lead to the most serious consequences, such as fines, lawsuits, negative publicity, business interruptions, and loss of clientele. These outcomes demonstrate the need to remain compliant to ensure the integrity and stability of organizations.

Cybersecurity compliance also helps in the creation of structures of governance by clarifying roles, responsibilities and processes revolving around security and compliance. This enhances communication among various departments and responsibility in the management of cybersecurity threats.

Depending on the industry and geographic location, organizations are most of the time required to adhere to several regulations frameworks at the same time. This adds complexity and necessitates constant monitoring and updating so that there can always be adherence with changing regulatory conditions.

Business Continuity and Operational Impact

Business continuity is a business strategy that helps companies anticipate, manage, and recover from disruptions to regular company operations by utilizing both people and technology. Business continuity planning includes disaster recovery, which is the process of resuming IT services after an unexpected interruption, but it doesn't end there. A business continuity plan's primary objective is to keep the company operational in the event of an unanticipated calamity, like an earthquake, or a planned one, such the implementation of a significant infrastructure update.

Business continuity planning is a procedure that is well-established and methodical in nature, and that defines how an organization would carry on with its operations and provide the necessary services in case of some unforeseen inconveniences like natural calamities, technology failures, or any other emergencies. It generally encompasses measures to protect the workers, maintain the most essential processes, and reduce financial and reputational losses, and the eventual objective is to swiftly restore and get back on the usual business operations.

Role of Cybersecurity in Business Continuity Planning

The risk of a cyberattack has never been higher due to organizations' growing reliance on digital technology. Cyberthreats like ransomware attacks, data breaches, and denial of service pose a threat to enterprises that might be just as catastrophic as a natural catastrophe. Due to their ability to tamper with critical data and disrupt corporate activities, these threats can result in significant financial and reputational damages. For this reason, a solid business continuity plan (BCP) must include cybersecurity.

An efficient and comprehensive approach to cybersecurity gives the company the resources it needs to carry out all crucial procedures, even during a crisis. Important areas of attention consist of:

- **Proactive Risk Management**

  The organizations need to be in a continual identify mode of the existence of vulnerabilities in their systems, processes, and networks. Through threat identification, businesses can put in place preventive measures that ensure that cyberattacks do not lead to a full-fledged crisis.

- **Data Protection**

  Business continuity is based on the protection of sensitive and critical data. By using control tools like encryption, multi-factor authentication and secure access control, it will be possible to make sure that in case of a breach, important information is still protected.

- **Disaster Recovery Planning**

  Hack attacks may lead to short- and long-term shutdowns. A clear disaster recovery plan enables companies to have IT systems, applications, and data back online as quickly as possible, which can reduce the recovery time and decrease the effects of an incident.

- **Continuous Monitoring**

  Network, endpoint, and application surveillance should be performed in real time in order to effectively identify and respond to a threat. The ongoing observation helps organizations to control the risks prior to their escalation so that the operations run in a smoother and safer situation during the critical times.

- **Implementation of Business Continuity Planning**

  In cybersecurity, business continuity planning (BCP) is a series of strategies to enable organizations to embed resilience strategies into their security system to guarantee that the organization can withstand and recover from the impact of any disruption associated with cyber incidents. It starts with a risk assessment to determine the possible threat of ransomware, insider threats, or system malfunctions, and plotting the consequences thereof on the key business processes. Once risks are identified.

Organizations will need to create policies and procedures that outline the way the important activities will be carried out in the event of an incident, with the assistance of such measures as data backups, disaster recovery procedures, and redundancy.

The process of testing, monitoring, and updating the BCP on a regular basis is necessary to make sure that it adapts to the emerging technologies, the changes in the organization, and the changes in the cyber threat environment.

The implementation of business continuity planning BCP together with cybersecurity protection measures enables organizations to maintain secure handling of confidential information while complying with regulatory standards and safeguarding their market reputation and customer trust during unexpected operational interruptions.

Challenges in Industry Adoption of Cybersecurity Frameworks

There are several challenges that organizations experience when implementing cybersecurity frameworks. Such challenges are usually motivated by emerging threats, humans, and the complexity of technology.

1. **Increasing Sophistication of Cyber Attacks**

   Cyber-attacks have reached unprecedented heights of sophistication, and they are extremely hard to detect and combat. Attackers gain access to a network and usually go undetected for months or even years, based on such techniques as Advanced Persistent Threats. In the process, they would have collected important information or made piecemeal disruptions to operations. Days have passed when ransomware was just an extremely simple threat; it has evolved into something that is even more complex. The bad actors are not limited to encryption of files, but they also impose a threat to leak sensitive information in instances where their demands are not fulfilled. This will paralyze businesses as no payment will be a guarantee of recovery, and in most cases, they will be exploited even further.

2. **Human Error**

   Human error is still as much of a problem when it comes to security breaches involving cybercrimes, and it is usually the weakest link in the security safeguards of organizations. Weak passwords, sharing of credentials between multiple accounts and phishing are some of the most prevalent errors. With all the sensitization efforts in place, phishing is one of the most effective tools used by cybercriminals, as a number of employees fall prey to the emails because they assume that they are authentic.

3. **Rapidly Evolving Technology**

   In terms of cybersecurity, the rapid advancement of technology has both benefits and drawbacks. While new technologies are more inventive and efficient, they also bring with them new vulnerabilities that hackers might take advantage of. By connecting both household appliances and industrial control systems, the Internet of Things has significantly expanded the attack surface. Because the majority of these gadgets were not designed with complete security in mind, attackers may readily access them. Similar to this, the advent of cloud computing has changed how businesses handle and store data, but it also has security issues of its own.

4. **Third-Party Risks**

   As third-party vendors and other partners are becoming more and more employed to handle and run most of the business operations, the aspect of risks, security breaches through these third-party agencies also increases accordingly. Although the relationship between a company and different third-party vendors is mandatory in carrying out the process of running a business, it can be very crucial to security in cases where the vendors fail to abide by the stringent parameters of security. A single third-party supplier will cause a possible chain effect throughout the supply chain.

5. **Insufficient Experts in Cybersecurity**

   One of the biggest challenges is the general dearth of skilled cybersecurity professionals. The need for competent cybersecurity specialists has never been greater due to the increasing frequency and complexity of cyber-attacks, but the required number of certified professionals has not kept up with this need. It is one of the skill gaps that cause companies to suffer because of their inability to recognize, mitigate, and respond to cyber-attacks.

MULTIPLE CHOICE QUESTIONS (MCQS)

1. **What is the primary purpose of a national cybersecurity framework?**

   A. To develop software applications

   B. To protect a nation's digital infrastructure and data

   C. To promote entertainment industries

   D. To increase internet speed

2. **Which of the following is a key component of national cybersecurity strategies?**

   A. Marketing plans

   B. Risk assessment and management

   C. Graphic design standards

   D. Hardware manufacturing

3. **What does the regulatory and compliance ecosystem ensure in cybersecurity?**

   A. Faster internet access

   B. Adherence to laws, standards, and guidelines

   C. Increased social media usage

   D. Development of games

4. **Which entity typically enforces cybersecurity regulations at the national level?**
   A. Private individuals
   B. Government agencies
   C. Local shops
   D. Schools only

5. **What is the main benefit of public–private partnerships (PPP) in cyber defense?**
   A. Reduced taxes
   B. Shared resources and threat intelligence
   C. Increased advertising
   D. Limited collaboration

6. **International cyber norms primarily aim to:**
   A. Promote cyber warfare
   B. Establish rules for responsible state behavior in cyberspace
   C. Limit internet access
   D. Ban technology usage

7. **Which organization plays a major role in global cybersecurity cooperation?**
   A. Local clubs
   B. International organizations like the United Nations
   C. Private banks only
   D. Retail companies

8. **What is risk governance in cybersecurity?**
   A. Ignoring cyber threats
   B. Managing and mitigating cybersecurity risks at a national level
   C. Designing websites
   D. Increasing bandwidth

9. **National resilience models focus on:**

   A. Preventing all cyber-attacks completely

   B. Recovering quickly from cyber incidents and maintaining operations

   C. Eliminating internet usage

   D. Limiting digital growth

10. **Which of the following best summarizes Chapter 2?**

    A. Cybersecurity is only a technical issue

    B. Cybersecurity requires policies, collaboration, and governance at national and international levels

    C. Only private companies handle cybersecurity

    D. Cybersecurity is not important

Answers

1	2	3	4	5	6	7	8	9	10
B	B	B	B	B	B	B	B	B	B

Chapter 3

CRITICAL INFRASTRUCTURE PROTECTION IN A HYPERCONNECTED WORLD

15. OVERVIEW

"Critical Infrastructure Protection" (CIP) in a hyperconnected world refers to the processes, technologies and policies implemented to prevent disruption, damage, or unauthorized access to critical infrastructure in the world. These infrastructures no longer stand alone; networks, cloud platforms, Internet of Things devices, and real-time data flow tie them all together to a large degree. Though this connectivity brings more efficiency, scalability and responsiveness, it also brings more attack surface and opens critical systems to cyber threats, system failures, and a cascade of disruption on a greater scale. Failure or a single attack on any industry can easily transfer the risk to other industries, raising the level of risk and potentially causing colossal social and economic consequences to society.

It is a very multidimensional environment, so defense against critical infrastructure must be multidimensional, incorporating cybersecurity, physical security, regulation, and other progressive knowledge such as artificial intelligence and predictive analytics. Governments and organizations should have a proactive approach to risk management policies, such as continuous monitoring, threat intelligence sharing, and resilience planning to be able to detect and respond within a short time to developing threats. Moreover, the partnership between the government and the business sector is important because a large part of the critical infrastructure is controlled and owned by the business sector. With the increased global interconnectedness, the CIP is moving towards resilience and adaptability rather than protection, whereby a system is not only capable of withstanding attacks and disruptions, but also able to heal fast and continue to provide the necessary services.

16. DEFINING CRITICAL INFRASTRUCTURE SECTORS

The buildings, resources, and systems that are essential to the operation of society and the economy are referred to as critical infrastructure. Some infrastructures are crucial because their interruption may affect public health, safety, security, or economic stability. Physical and virtual components that are interconnected and dependent on one another make up critical infrastructure.

Most countries and governing organizations enforce rules regarding the management of essential infrastructure. For instance, policies and procedures for the management and protection of critical infrastructure are established by US government organizations such as the Department of Homeland Security, the Cybersecurity and Infrastructure Security Agency, and the Department of Energy. Presidential Policy Directive 21 promotes a national effort to strengthen and preserve vital infrastructure that is safe, functional, and resilient.

The most recent rules, best practices, and technological advancements for maintaining the health of critical infrastructure must be understood by people in charge of such systems. We are surrounded by critical infrastructure sectors:

- The energy industry includes pipelines, fuel storage, oil and natural gas infrastructure, nuclear reactors, and electricity grids.
- Chemical industry: production of petrochemicals, distribution of chemicals, and agricultural chemicals.
- Transportation sector: public transportation networks, railroads, highways, bridges, airports, and seaports.

- Sewage, pumping stations, reservoirs, dams, and water treatment facilities are examples of water and wastewater systems.
- The communications industry includes satellite systems, internet service providers, and telecommunication networks.
- The clearinghouses, banks, stock exchanges, and payment systems are all part of the financial services sector.
- Healthcare: Medical supply networks, clinics, and hospitals.
- Emergency services: emergency management systems, police, and fire departments.
- Food and agriculture: farms, food processing facilities, circulation systems, and food safety systems.
- Government: Federal buildings, defense industrial bases, and national security systems.
- Technology related to information includes internet infrastructure, cybersecurity systems, data centers, and essential hardware and software.

Due to the interdependence of these infrastructures, events in one area may have a wide-ranging impact on other sectors.

Common threats to critical infrastructure

Critical infrastructure is threatened by a variety of events that may interfere with its functioning and create risks to the safety of the masses, national economic growth and security. Typical dangers consist of:

- **Cyberattacks:** To obtain unapproved access, disrupt business, pilfer private information, and/or cause physical injury, attackers may also attempt to access control systems, networks, and software vulnerabilities.
- **Physical attacks:** Vandalism, terrorism, and sabotage can endanger lives, interfere with or disrupt activities, and directly harm facilities. Businesses, transportation networks, critical

manufacturing processes, and other resources may be the target of these attacks.

- **Natural catastrophes:** Hurricanes, earthquakes, flooding, wildfires, and extreme weather can all have an impact on essential services. Historical climatic patterns may create problems with systems relying on historical patterns as extreme weather events become more frequent and intense.
- **Pandemics and health emergencies:** Outbreaks of diseases and pandemics may lead to shortages of workforce, disruptions in operations and high demand, straining the system and the overall resilience of public health responders.
- **Weaknesses in the supply chain:** The supply chain may have vulnerabilities, including compromised or counterfeit products, which may create areas of weakness that can be leveraged to disrupt operations or lead to system compromises.
- **Dependencies on technology:** The more our critical infrastructure is interconnected and depends on sophisticated technologies, the more we are dependent on more complicated systems and software.

Protecting critical infrastructure is a complex task, which involves strong cybersecurity, disaster preparedness and response, robust design of critical infrastructure, security of the supply chain, partnership and cooperation between the public and private, and continuous monitoring and evaluation of risks.

How to manage critical infrastructure

The management of critical infrastructure is done through the implementation of reliable software programs and systems that oversee, protect, and manage the various infrastructure components.

- **Asset management:** To keep an eye on all of your vital infrastructure assets, including network devices, software licensing, and physical equipment, use software-based "enterprise asset management" (EAM) systems. This makes asset inventory, maintenance, and lifecycle management more efficient.

- **"Supervisory Control and Data Acquisition" (SCADA) and control systems:** To monitor and manage the physical operations of vital infrastructure, provide SCADA systems or comparable control systems. These systems are used to collect real-time data, make choices, and remotely monitor and manage the infrastructure.
- **Network security and monitoring:** To continuously monitor the network infrastructure, use security and network monitoring tools. This helps detect and address any cyberthreats, vulnerabilities, or anomalies that can compromise the availability and integrity of vital infrastructure systems.
- **Risk-based approaches:** These strategies entail evaluating and prioritizing infrastructure system hazards, the development of risk management actions and the distribution of resources according to the priority of assets and the severity of any disruption.
- **Data analytics and predictive maintenance:** With the help of computer analytical tools, analyze the data obtained in the work with the key infrastructure systems. With data analytics, one can detect patterns and trends and implement predictive maintenance, which allows them to stem equipment malfunctions and encourage downtime correction.
- **Remote monitoring and control:** Using software solutions, describe the features of remote monitoring and control. This allows operators to monitor and manage critical infrastructure systems from a single location, reducing the requirement for physical presence at every location and enabling timely incident response.
- **Disaster recovery and incident response:** Using software tools, create thorough incident response plans and catastrophe recovery techniques. These plans should include detailed instructions on what to do in the event of a cyberattack,

natural disaster, or another emergency. The response and recovery procedures can be made more efficient with the use of software-based incident management solutions.

- **Regulatory requirements and compliance:** Verify that the software programs used to manage vital organization adhere to all applicable laws and guidelines. This covers industry-specific compliance requirements, data protection laws, and cybersecurity standards.
- **Training and education:** Employees in charge of using software to manage vital infrastructure should receive instruction and training. It is crucial to make sure that administrators and operators are knowledgeable about cybersecurity best practices and protocols, as well as the software tools and systems in use.
- **Redundancy and backup systems:** Put redundancy and backup systems in place to guarantee that crucial operations continue. This covers data backup options, backup power supply, and redundant servers. Regular testing of backup systems is necessary to guarantee their efficacy.
- **Cooperation and info exchange:** Encourage cooperation and information exchange amongst important infrastructure players, including governmental bodies, business associates, and cybersecurity groups. This contributes to the overall resilience and security of critical infrastructure and helps spread threat intelligence, best practices, and lessons learned.
- **Public-private collaborations:** Information sharing, coordinated responses, and resource distribution to threats and disruptions are made possible by projects and partnerships involving organizations in the public and private sectors. The patterns highlight how critical infrastructure management is evolving, which has seen a shift in focus to novel methods, technology, teamwork and proactive application of risk and resilience.

The approach to managing critical infrastructure using software needs to cover observation, management, safety, upkeep, and adherence. Critical infrastructure could be effectively controlled with software solutions, ensuring its dependability, security, and resilience.

17. THREATS TO ENERGY, FINANCE, AND HEALTHCARE SYSTEMS

Geopolitical and technological factors are contributing to the increase in cyberattacks on the energy sector. Cases of ransomware attacks have increased significantly, and various organizations have reported security breaches across the energy, oil, gas and utilities sectors. Although most of these attacks have been directed at IT settings, the risk to critical operational technology (OT) networks is growing quickly (Ovabor et al., 2024).

Ransomware is not the only aspect of a threat. Attackers motivated by ideology and hacktivist groups are increasingly targeting energy companies, and frequently publicize suspected breaches to earn credibility. What is more worrying is that more and more nation-state actors are becoming involved with countries like China, Iran, and North Korea, who are now focusing on energy infrastructure and staff to carry out cyber-espionage activities.

All these cyber threats are mostly based on geopolitical conflicts, such as the continuous global conflicts and power struggles among nations. This, in turn, has made critical energy infrastructure one of the priority targets to showcase cyber capabilities. Though most attacks have been aimed at espionage, the possibility of disruptive or destructive cyber operations is a serious concern.

The development of technologies has also increased the attack surface in the energy industry. Energy networks have become more vulnerable to the convergence of IT and OT systems and the growing use of industrial Internet of Things and cloud computing devices. Attackers tend to use IT systems as a point of entry to more sensitive OT environments.

Hacking into OT systems could be very costly since the attackers are able to interfere with or stop energy production processes. This will give leverage to higher demands in the case of ransomware and in the worst case, it might cause physical destruction and threats to human life.

The threat landscape has also changed due to the swift adoption of artificial intelligence. Although AI does have some benefits to operations, it also creates new vulnerabilities and opens the door to more advanced cyberattacks. Moreover, the rise in digitalization has contributed to the appearance of more vulnerable points in power grids and, therefore, made them more vulnerable to cyber-attacks.

Ransomware Attacks and Data Breaches in the Energy Sector

One of the biggest risks to the energy sector is thought to be ransomware attacks. Another interesting case is the Ransom Hub assault on Halliburton in August 2024, which cost the company to the tune of about 35 million dollars as the company was compelled to shut down IT systems and disconnect customers. This is the financial and operational effect ransomware can have on large energy organizations, as such incidents indicate.

The ecosystem of ransomware is still delivering changes, as threat actors are allied and moving to ransomware-as-a-service (RaaS). As an example, the shift of Ransom Hub to Dragon Force infrastructure signifies the growing cooperation between cybercriminal gangs, and attacks have become more advanced and difficult to thwart.

Breachage of data involving energy-related organizations is another indicator of the magnitude of the threat. In 2024, Dragon Force took responsibility for a breach of a 2024 intrusion into Ikav Energy that resulted in the leakage of approximately 177 GB of security-related personal data and information. Though it was not a direct blow at the very bases of energy infrastructure, such cases demonstrate the power of third-party and supply chain vulnerability risks.

Energy and nuclear-related organizations are also the targets of ransomware groups. Cyber-attacks on organizations, including the Brazilian state-owned nuclear organization NUCLEP, included efforts to sell massive amounts of stolen data and high ransom fees. Such cases suggest that attackers are now targeting sensitive research and development information to rake in as much financial gain as possible.

Moreover, there have been several data breaches related to organizations working in the energy industry connected to such well-known ransomware organizations as ClOP and Hellcat. Such attacks usually leverage breaches in supply-chain systems, and this is the case with the MOVEit-related attacks, where information of many energy companies was disclosed by using the third-party platforms that were compromised.

In general, ransomware incidents in the energy industry are increasingly more organized, financially-oriented and selective. Direct intrusions, third-party intrusions, and the constantly changing networks of cybercriminals have combined to make ransomware a material and increasingly important threat to the energy infrastructure and the organizations that support it.

Importance of Cybersecurity in Financial Services

The following are some of the reasons why cybersecurity is important to financial services companies:

- **Sensitive Data Protection**

  Names, addresses, credit card numbers, social security numbers, and transaction histories of customers are just a few examples of the highly personal financial information that financial institutions handle. Customers are not the only ones who value this data, but also cybercriminals who use it to commit fraud.

  There are several financial services technologies that organizations use to safeguard sensitive financial data. Cybersecurity offers encryption and a secure network, as well as effective authentication procedures that can only grant authorized access to individuals and systems. It also offers the means of identifying and reacting, minimizing the possible impact and preventing any illegal access or data breaches.

- **Prevention of Financial Loss**

  Cyber-attacks are potentially very costly. Cybercriminals can also loot bank accounts and commit fraudulent transactions with stolen credit cards, but data breaches may also lead to regulatory fines, legal expenses, and a bad reputation. In the financial services sector, the price of cybercrime is rising.

  Financial services cybersecurity plays a key role in loss prevention. Financial institutions can prevent and reduce the effects of cyber-attacks through malware, intrusion detection systems, network security, and other cybersecurity measures.

- **Maintaining Consumer Trust**

  In the financial services industry, the industry's core component is trust. Customers trust financial organizations to handle their funds and private data. Any violation of this trust, such as a successful cyberattack or data breach, would be disastrous to the reputation and customer relations of a financial institution.

  Cybersecurity within the financial service environment assists in upholding consumer trust by safeguarding financial transactions and customer data. It makes customers believe that their information and money are secure, which builds trust in the services provided by the financial institution.

- **Regulatory Compliance**

  The financial industry has a strict regulatory context that dictates the rules and regulations that need to be adhered to in order to secure and maintain the safety of the financial systems and safeguard consumers. Among these, there are the "Bank Secrecy Act" (BSA), Dodd-Frank Act, "Sarbanes-Oxley Act" (SOX) and the "Payment Card Industry Data Security Standard" (PCI DSS), among others.

  These laws require an array of cybersecurity. Indicatively, the "Payment Card Industry Data Security Standard" (PCI-DSS) mandates companies to protect the cardholder data, ensure that the access control measures are strong, there is an information security policy and that networks are tested and monitored on a regular basis.

Common Cybersecurity Threats in Financial Services

- **Phishing and Social Engineering Attacks**

  The financial services industry is also susceptible to cybersecurity risks like social engineering and phishing. Cybercriminals trick victims into disclosing private or monetary data in these attacks, which they achieve by pretending to be an authority figure. They could send an email, for example, claiming to be the bank of the individual requesting them to change their interpretation information or to confirm a payment.

  A couple of cybersecurity solutions can be used to reduce such attacks. These involve informing customers of the danger of phishing and social engineering scams, using multi-factor authentication and email filtering software to prevent phishing emails to ensure that even with stolen logins, one cannot be an unauthorized user.

- **Malware and Ransomware**

  Another type of cybersecurity threat common to the financial services industry is malware, such as ransomware. Malware refers to harmful software that has the potential to interfere with the functioning of computers, collect important data, or orchestrate unapproved access to computer networks. One type of malware is ransomware. which causes encryption of files within a system and requires a ransom to be decrypted.

  Strong malware can solve these threats. It involves regularly installing and maintaining antivirus software, keeping an eye on network traffic to spot malware, patching and updating systems to fix vulnerabilities, and regularly backing up data to prevent ransomware attacks.

- **Distributed Denial of Service (DDoS) Attacks**

  A Distributed Denial of Service (DDoS) attack involves attacking a traffic-filled network, service, or infrastructure and making it unavailable. DDoS attacks may be used to disrupt the services of financial institutions, incur financial losses, or to distract the activities of the attackers in the process of breaking into their systems.

  The financial services companies may fight against the DDoS attacks in several ways. These involve the use of DDoS protection systems that are able to identify and curb DDoS requests, the use of redundant systems to ensure service in the event of an attack, and the preparation of DDoS attacks in order to make sure the event is effectively respondent.

- **Insider Threats**

  Cybersecurity threats that are associated with insiders are defined as insider threats. Those may be the employees, the contractors, or anybody else who has been given permission to access the schemes and the data of the institution. The insider threats may be especially difficult to deal with because such persons can be given access legitimately and may be familiar with the processes and systems of the institution.

  Financial services companies pay attention to access control, monitoring, and training in order to minimize the risk of insider threats. It also makes sure that people can only access the data and systems they require to work, detects abnormal or suspicious activity, and educates employees about how to identify and address cybersecurity risks.

- **API Vulnerabilities**

  In the financial sector, API is used to facilitate integration among systems and services. Nonetheless, cyber criminals can use APIs to access systems and data without authorization in case of their insecurity.

The API vulnerabilities may be overcome with the help of secure coding, frequent API security gateways and security testing. The other important metric is to track API activity and identify and address the symptoms of a breach.

Common Cyber Threats in the Healthcare Industry

Healthcare is a sensitive sector with a multifaceted cybersecurity threat that endangers patient care and the integrity of the system. The next active threats serve to take advantage of the weaknesses to interfere with functions and steal confidential information, and are highly dangerous to the systems of an organization. Additional vulnerabilities in the current medical devices open loopholes that attackers take advantage of to compromise patient safety.

Phishing assaults: Phishing is one of the most common and damaging attacks against your healthcare organization. The "Healthcare Information and Management Systems Society" (HIMSS) found the following number of security incidents related to the different types of phishing in their Healthcare Cybersecurity Survey, which was carried out in November and December of 2024:

- General email phishing - 63%
- SMS phishing - 34%
- Spear phishing - 34%
- Business email compromise (BEC) - 31%
- Phishing websites - 21%
- Malicious ads - 20%
- Social media phishing - 19%
- Vishing (voicemail phishing) - 17%
- Whaling (also known as executive impersonation) - 16%

Phishing's prominence as a leading cybersecurity threat to your healthcare organization underscores the urgent need for comprehensive defenses. The numerous types of phishing attacks require solid training of employees, sophisticated threat detection software and supervised access control to secure sensitive patient information and ensure compliance with one of your regulatory requirements.

Ransomware and Malware: Malware and ransomware pose a serious risk since they can shut down entire hospital systems, disrupt patient care, and expose enormous volumes of PHI. The healthcare industry is a sector especially susceptible because it is a life-or-death kind of business, thus it is a good target for criminals involved in cybercrime.

In a report of 2024, the Office of Information Security and the "Health Sector Cybersecurity Coordination Center" (HC3) of the HHS indicated that over 460 U.S. healthcare organizations were targeted by attacks by groups including LockBit, ClOp, ALPHV, and Bian Lian (among others). During a single massive attack against a vast network of hospitals, more than 500,000 patients were affected in various ways, including delays in care and appointments as well as ambulance diversion. EHR was taken off, and paper records had to be used. The patient portal and payroll were broken. The damage amounted to USD 100 million all in all.

Insider Threats: Insider threats, whether deliberate or unintentional, are a serious threat to healthcare organizations. Security may be breached by Workers, independent contractors, and outside suppliers who gain access to sensitive systems like EHRs that store PHI due to careless data management, unauthorized disclosure or intentional malpractices. Such threats increase the susceptibility of the growing attack surface in the field of healthcare caused by the implementation of EHRs and IoMT devices.

The aftermath of insider-related events is huge, such as information leaks, business downtime, and legal fines within the framework of HIPAA, GDPR, PIPEDA, NDB, and other international regulations. The measures that healthcare organizations must take to reduce these risks are to enact strict access control, an effective monitoring system and extensive security awareness training based on the high-stress environments of such organizations.

Hacked Medical Implantation: The increased connectivity of medical equipment, including imaging devices, IV infusion pumps, and patient monitors, has transformed the healthcare system by making it possible to integrate real-time data and providing remote patient care. These IoMT devices are integrated with the EHRs and the hospital networks to improve medical effectiveness and patient care.

But this connectivity is causing new attack vectors to threat actors as well as posing a lot of cybersecurity risks. The IoMT devices are prone to exploits because a lot of them use old software or do not have strong encryption. Indicatively, unpatched systems may be compromised in a phishing attack or a direct network intrusion that may expose the data stored in EHRs. Not only can such weaknesses cause breach of data, but also jeopardize the safety of patients, since hackers can use devices to change dosages of medication or falsify vital signs with either disastrous or even life-threatening clinical outcomes.

Cybersecurity Solutions for Financial Services

Cybersecurity solutions that are available to financial institutions are used to safeguard their services and client information from online threats. The most important defensive strategies are as follows:

1. **Web Application Firewalls**

   The WAF is a defensive layer that is installed between the Internet and the web application. It remains between packets of data entering and leaving a web application or website and blocks, filters and monitors these packets of data. Through a WAF, financial institutions will be able to prevent the common attacks on the internet, which include cross-site scripting, SQL injection and brute force attacks.

   A WAF uses a collection of regulations known as policies. These policies stipulate what cannot be passed through traffic and what can go through the traffic. Financial institutions should constantly revise such policies to be ahead of threats that arise. Periodic security audits may assist in identifying areas of weakness and revising the WAF policies.

2. **DDoS Protection**

   In a DDoS attack, attackers flood a system, network, or server with Internet traffic. This may result into slowing of services or the crashing down of services, thereby disabling the operations of a business to an extent.

   Financial institutions can use DDoS protection solutions to reduce the threat of DDoS assaults. These tools keep an eye on network traffic and spot unusual surges that can point to a DDoS attack. Suspicious traffic is redirected off the network by the DDoS protection program when it has been identified, hence reducing the impact.

3. **Anti-Fraud and Web Fraud Prevention.**

   Online fraud in the financial services industry is very common. Fraudsters can obtain important financial information in a number of ways, including phishing, identity theft, and card fraud. Anti-fraud technologies help financial organizations prevent and identify fraud.

   These solutions utilize sophisticated algorithms of machine learning and analytics to identify questionable trends and behaviors, which could be identified as an indicator of fraud. Financial institutions can address financial crimes by preventing fraud in real-time, which will help in avoiding losses of money.

4. **Identity and Access Management (IAM)**

   "Identity and access management" (IAM) is a business process architecture that makes managing electronic identities easier. It contains the technologies needed to make identity management easier, such as user provisioning, "single sign-on" (SSO), and "multi-factor authentication" (MFA).

   IAM provides the right people with the right resources at the right moments and for the right reasons. It is also essential for preventing unauthorized access to sensitive data and systems. IAM is able to be used by financial institutions to have stringent access controls, thus reducing the chances of data breaches to the bare minimum.

5. **State-of-the-Art Threat Protection Solutions.**

   Analytics for dangerous activity, network security, email security, and endpoint protection are just a few of the technologies used in ATP solutions to detect and stop sophisticated cyberthreats.

   These solutions offer automated response and real-time intelligence of threats. The ATP solutions are important towards protecting the financial institutions against sophisticated cyber threats by being able to identify and reduce risks before they have a chance to hurt the institutions.

6. **Vulnerability Assessment and Penetration Testing (VAPT).**

   VAPT refers to the process of detecting, estimating, and prioritizing system vulnerabilities. It is an overall analysis that identifies vulnerabilities and risks of a system.

   VAPT, in terms of the financial services context, assists in securing important data, deterring breaches of data, and ensuring compliance with regulations. It is a preemptive measure towards cybersecurity, in which the possible threats are recognized and removed before they may cause any damage.

7. **Security Awareness and Training Programs**

   Even the best cybersecurity systems are useless if end users are not aware of cyberthreats and how to counter them. The security awareness and training program's goal is to inform users about the different types of cyberthreats, how they operate, and the most effective defenses against them.

   These training programs are crucial in the financial services sector. They provide users of digital financial solutions with trust in addition to helping to secure sensitive financial information.

8. **Data Activity Monitoring**

   Hacking or inappropriate use of data can have catastrophic consequences for the banking sector. Every operation in a database is monitored and recorded in real time by a system known as data activity monitoring.

   Monitoring data activity in the financial services sector adds another level of security. It aids in protecting from internal and external threats, which are frequently disregarded. The data is consistent with the financial data's secrecy and integrity since all the data activities are put under close supervision.

9. **Data Risk Analytics**

   One cybersecurity preventive strategy is data risk analytics. It comprises the study of the information to determine possible risks and threats. This is carried out with the help of sophisticated algorithms and machine learning that is able to identify any trends and abnormalities that can show a cyber threat.

   Analytics for data risk might be a tactical benefit in the framework of financial services. It can be proactively managed by anticipating the possibility of future risks. It is also useful in ensuring compliance with regulations since it gives an objective evaluation of the risks of data.

18. INDUSTRIAL CONTROL SYSTEMS AND SCADA SECURITY

The "Supervisory Control and Data Acquisition" (SCADA) and "Industrial Control Systems" (ICS) are significant in the control and management of industrial operations in energy, manufacturing, water treatment, and transportation of the industrial industry. These systems are charged with the responsibility of supervising the physical operations, machinery operators and ensuring the efficient operation of important infrastructure. However, with the growing levels of digitalization and connectivity, cyber-attacks have been witnessed on ICS and SCADA systems. The systems were originally intended to be deployed in isolated settings and were not engineered at such a high level of cybersecurity to be easy targets for hackers with malicious intentions of inflicting chaos on the services offered.

Information Technology and Operational Technology network convergence is one of the biggest security problems in ICS and SCADA environments. As much as this integration enhances efficiency and real-time access to data, it has the side effect of widening the attacker surface, which a cybercriminal can use to exploit vulnerabilities in interconnected systems. IT networks are frequently the entry point of threat actors who, at a later point in time, break into OT environments to modify control processes. Also, the utilization of outdated systems, the absence of regular updates, and a small number of authentication procedures contribute to an even greater threat of unauthorized access and system vulnerability.

To secure the ICS and SCADA systems, a multi-layered approach is necessary and extensive. Companies should also establish effective access control, network segmentation, monitoring and continuous detection of intrusion systems to secure the vital infrastructure. Security checks, patching and staff training should also be done regularly in order to mitigate vulnerability and avoid attacks. Moreover, modernizing cybersecurity frameworks and standards will enable organizations to reinforce their security systems against the ever-changing threats. Since the number of cyberattacks on critical infrastructure is steadily increasing, protecting ICS and SCADA systems has become the primary concern in ensuring the stability of operations and the safety of the population.

Common ICS security challenges

- **External threats and targeted attacks**

  External threats in ICS security refer to risks originating outside the organization or industrial environment that may jeopardize the availability, confidentiality, or integrity of ICS components. Common external threats include malware and ransomware, phishing attacks, nation-state actors, hacktivists, insider threats with external influence, supply chain attacks, and more.

- **Internal threats**

  Internal threats in ICS security refer to risks posed by individuals or processes within the organization or facility that can compromise the security, safety, or functionality of the system. These threats may be both unintentional and intentional and are important since insiders usually have direct access and privileged information to critical systems. Common examples include malicious insiders, errors caused by well-meaning employees, or third-party risks from vendors, suppliers, or even maintenance personnel.

- **Human error**

  Human error refers to mistakes or oversights by employees, operators, or other individuals that compromise the safety, security, or functionality of ICS environments. Examples include configuration errors, improper patching, neglecting security protocols, unauthorized device usage, and/or data entry errors.

- **High availability requirements**

  ICS systems need to maintain functionality and accessibility despite device malfunctions, software problems, cyberattacks, or other disturbances. To have high availability, ICS systems need to plan for redundancy, failover mechanisms, disaster recovery, patch management without downtime, cyber resilience, monitoring and alerts, secure communication, and more.

- **Insecure proprietary protocols**

  Insecure proprietary protocols in ICS security are common. Legacy devices and machines—all with their own protocols—lack modern security features like encryption, authentication, and integrity verification. These protocols were often designed for reliability and real-time performance in isolated environments; however, never designed for security in connected or internet-facing environments.

- **Focus on detection over prevention**

  ICS security is sometimes set up to identify threats rather than prevent them. This is because ICS demands high availability because there is a serious concern that legitimate activities could be hindered.

ICS security best practices

Best practices for ICS security ensure protection of critical infrastructure and operations from cyberthreats, human error, and operational disruptions. These practices focus on security "operational technology" (OT) and "information technology" (IT) to minimize vulnerabilities and ensure resilient operations.

- **Network segmentation**

  Isolating ICS from IT networks physically and logically can help limit exposure to external threats. Oftentimes, this is achieved using "demilitarized zones" (DMZs) to control traffic flow between ICS and external networks.

- **Access control and user authentication**

  Best practice is to adhere to the least privilege principle, meaning that access should be limited to the minimum required for the role of the user, ensuring operators only have access to what they need to perform their tasks.

- **Secure remote access**

  Limiting and securing remote access is considered a best practice for ICS security. This includes using VPNs with encryption, limiting remote access to only when necessary, and also monitoring remote sessions.

- **Regular patch management**

  Timely deployment of patches ensures software and hardware are updated to fix vulnerabilities and security flaws. Firmware on ICS devices, including controllers, sensors, and other field devices, is strongly recommended.

- **Secure communication protocols**

  Leveraging secure protocols for data transmission within ICS networks protects against eavesdropping and tampering.

Where possible, transition to secure versions of legacy protocols (e.g., OPC UA, MQTT) that offer encryption and/or authentication.

System Architecture of SCADA

A SCADA system's architecture is multifaceted, with each layer being essential to the system's overall effectiveness and usefulness. The five different layers are broken out as follows:

- **The First Layer (Field Devices):** The SCADA system is built on this layer. It is made up of field-based sensors and actuators. Temperature, pressure, flow rate, and other environmental or process data are all read by sensors. On the other hand, actuators are those that respond to commands by doing things like turning on a motor or opening or closing a valve.
- **The Second Layer (Field Controllers):** "Remote Terminal Units" (RTUs) and "Programmable Logic Controllers" (PLCs) are the local controllers that make up this tier. These are the devices that are directly connected to the actuators and sensors. They send control signals to the actuators after receiving data from the sensors. Primary data processing and swiftly and automatically adapting to changes in field conditions are related to RTUs and PLCs.
- **The Third Layer (Local Supervisory):** Local supervisory equipment makes up this layer. They provide a more centralized place for control and monitoring by collecting and centralizing the data provided by the field controllers. This layer handles more intricate analysis and judgment based on the total evidence and can give the field controllers more precise instructions.
- **The Fourth Layer (Production Control):** Numerous local supervision systems make up this layer. It collects data on various systems and has a broader role in operations management. The goal of this layer is to produce reports and information that are crucial for strategic decision-making, production management, and efficiency analysis.

- **The Fifth Layer (Main Monitoring Station):** The main monitoring station is the highest point in the SCADA architecture. This incorporates the SCADA computer system that controls all the processes occurring. It acts as a center for collecting data, controlling processes, system analysis and making high-level decisions. This layer guarantees the overall functionality of the whole SCADA system, ensuring that the entire system is well monitored, which allows its operators a clear picture of the system configuration and allows them to make informed decisions about the system.

All the levels of the SCADA system architecture are thoroughly designed to coordinate with one another and provide efficient data flow, quick reaction to changes and successful control of the whole system. This type of hierarchy enables localized control within the lower level and centralized supervision at higher levels, which makes SCADA systems very adaptable and efficient in managing intricate industrial operations.

Benefits of Modern SCADA

1. **Remote Monitoring and Control**

   The current SCADA systems provide operators with the ability to control and observe machinery and procedures irrespective of their physical location. This not only makes the operations easy and does not require manual intervention, but also solves the issues faster. It is the opportunity to remotely monitor and manage processes through the internet connection that creates great flexibility of operations and cost saving in traveling and managing the processes on location.

2. **Improved Efficiency**

   The SCADA systems can be used to give real-time information, which can then be used to identify and resolve the problems as they occur and hence reduce the downtime and effects of problems. Robotic activities improve work efficiency. As an example, the use of energy in the manufacturing process may be optimized, which means consuming less and spending less. Constant monitoring of processes would result in the correction and detection of inefficiencies, which would enhance performance.

3. **Real-time Data Collection**

   Real-time gathering and evaluation of data is priceless to the SCADA systems. The constant monitoring of processes and equipment allows for obtaining current information that is critical to making informed decisions. This information can be applied to decrease downtime, optimize processes, and enhance product quality. Long-term data analysis and storage reveal patterns, improve investments, and new improvements in the future.

4. **Cost Savings**

   SCADA systems offer a great contribution in terms of reducing cost through decreasing downtime and improving efficiency. Problems are identified and fixed within a short period; hence, lost productions are minimized as well as repair expenses. Operation costs are also reduced by energy optimization and process improvement. The analysis of real-time data helps in the detection and rectification of inefficiencies, which will lead to further savings as time goes by.

5. **Enhanced Safety**

   By providing real-time measurement of critical equipment and process characteristics, SCADA systems improve safety in various sectors. The identification of safety hazards in a timely manner will allow taking corrective measures that will minimize the occurrence of accidents and incidents. Whereas, in sectors such as chemicals, it is important to monitor parameters such as pressure and temperature in real-time, a better way of managing a safety situation is in the management of hazardous chemicals.

6. **Improved Quality**

   The application of SCADA systems offers actual data and control provisions, resulting in high product quality and consistency. This is due to continuous monitoring, where deviations are corrected immediately, eliminating the chances of producing poor quality.

The processes are also automated to provide quality control, hence ensuring stringent requirements for the production.

7. **Increased Productivity**

SCADA systems help in enhancing productivity through process control and automation. The automation minimizes the manpower, quickens the operation and enhances production. With better management of the processes and less downtime, there are direct results on the increased level of productivity, and organizations were able to accomplish more within less time.

8. **Scalability**

SCADA systems are flexible, and thus they can be used in businesses whose processes or equipment have variable requirements. Scalability is provided through the capacity to easily integrate with other systems and adjust to new procedures and equipment. Because of this, SCADA is the ideal way for businesses of all sizes to support expansion and transformation.

9. **Customization**

Any SCADA system can be customized to suit the requirements of any kind of organization. While the user interface can be customized, the digital component consists of software settings that allow for specific process monitoring and control, conveniently adjusted to be user-friendly. This degree of customization streamlines the processes and makes them more efficient, and it represents a huge benefit over non-specific options that are readily available.

10. **Data Management**

When it comes to long-term data storage, analysis, and reporting, SCADA systems are superior. The ability to handle large volumes of real-time data provides a comprehensive view of the equipment and process performance. In-depth study of the machinery and processes will be made easier by the sophisticated reporting, which will help with data-driven decision-making, process optimization, and effectiveness.

SCADA Security Best Practices

Because of the potential hazards, it is impossible to be certain that "Supervisory Control and Data Acquisition" (SCADA) systems are secure. Some of the most important recommended practices for guaranteeing SCADA security are as follows:

Map All Current Systems

The initial step towards strong security is to make a full map of the whole SCADA network. This comprises:

- **Connection Documentation:** Recording every point at which the system is connected to internal networks and the internet.
- **Component Inventory:** Keeping a running account of every piece of SCADA system hardware, software, firmware, and applications.
- **Access Control:** Recording the people who access different elements, particularly applications.
- **Detecting Data Entry and Exit Points:** It will assist in the identification of all the possible access points by which malware and external intrusions can occur.

Institute Monitoring and Detection

To identify potential threats and vulnerabilities, it's critical to deploy effective monitoring and detectors. Important tactics consist of:

- **Network Segmentation:** SCADA networks should be kept apart from other crucial business systems in order to prevent any attacks from spreading.
- **Physical and Cybersecurity Congruence:** To combat both physical and cyber threats, physical security and cybersecurity procedures should be coordinated.
- **Security Measures:** Use firewalls, unidirectional gateways, and application whitelisting to create a multi-layered defensive posture for SCADA networks.

Create Procedures for Network Security

Continuous security attention is essential to the integrity of SCADA security systems. This comprises:

- **Regular Security Checks:** Performing audits of security and keeping an eye out for anomalies in reports.
- **Standard Security Protocols:** Developing and putting into practice standard operating procedures for all users of SCADA networks.
- **Ongoing Assessments:** Regular Assessments of assets, vulnerabilities, and risks are required to keep security measures current and adaptable in the face of evolving threats.

Ensuring Continuous Improvement

- **Adaptive Security Measures:** To combat emerging threats, security measures should be updated and improved on a steady foundation.
- **Employee Education:** Ensuring that all staff members receive sufficient instruction in security knowledge and best practices.
- **Incident Response Planning:** Creating and keeping up a successful incident response strategy to take prompt action in the case of a security breach.

Leveraging Technology and Expertise

- **Advanced Security technology:** Protecting the SCADA systems with cutting-edge security tools and technology.
- **Cooperation with Security professionals:** To keep ahead of potential security threats and weaknesses, collaborate with cybersecurity professionals.

19. SUPPLY CHAIN VULNERABILITIES

Supply chain vulnerability is a term used to describe the vulnerability of a supply chain network to disruption, threat, or failure, potentially affecting business adversely. These weaknesses may exist in any of the stages, such as sourcing of raw materials, industrial, conveyance, circulation, and the final delivery.

A weak supply chain does not have the strength to handle and rebound fast in case of unforeseen problems, resulting in operational, financial, and reputation losses. These risks have also been increased due to the growing complexity and digitalization of supply chains globally, which are even more challenging to handle.

It has been shown that the worldwide supply chain is very sensitive and that disruptions in the supply chain can easily affect business, causing losses up to 45 percent of annual profits in a ten-year span. Consequently, supply chain vulnerabilities have become critical to determine and mitigate to achieve operational resiliency and long-term sustainability.

Along with structural vulnerabilities, the external factors that tend to affect the supply chain vulnerability include geopolitical tensions, natural disasters, and financial instabilities. The flow of goods and materials can be slowed down and be costly because of events such as trade restrictions, pandemics, or regional conflicts. Companies with few suppliers or having a small area or geographical location are highly vulnerable to these risks and hence diversification is a significant option in minimizing vulnerability.

The technological risks are also important contributors to the contemporary supply chain vulnerabilities. With a growing digitization of supply chains, Supply chains are more susceptible to data breaches, cyberattacks, and system failures. One cyberattacks on any logistics or supplier partner has the potential of creating crashes in the entire network, causing failure in operations. That is why, the adoption of effective cybersecurity and real-time monitoring, as well as risk management tactics, is necessary to make supply chain operations resilient and secure.

Why Is Understanding Supply Chain Vulnerability Important?

It is important that you know your vulnerabilities in the supply chain because:

- **Risk Mitigation:** Risk mitigation involves finding vulnerabilities so that you can devise effective strategies to mitigate risks before they happen.
- **Business Continuity:** A robust supply chain helps to maintain operations even in the face of unforeseen events or crises.
- **Competitive Advantage:** A business with a solid supply chain risk management procedure can respond to market shifts and disruptions more quickly than its competitors.
- **Cost Control:** Management of vulnerabilities (proactive) will prevent expensive emergency actions and losses incurred as a result of operational failures.
- **Stakeholder Confidence:** Resilience in supply chains instills confidence with customers, investors, and partners.

When an incident does occur, businesses with established supply chain risk management procedures see fewer interruptions and recover faster. Since then, supply chain vulnerability assessment has emerged as one of the pillars of operational excellence in the shipping and logistics sector in particular.

Understanding Supply Chain Attack Types

Supply chain attacks can be of various types, but three main and the most widespread ones deserve particular attention:

- **Software Attacks:** The hackers embed malicious source code into a trusted application in the software of the vendor. Also, in some instances, an update server could be compromised, and the attacker can use it to substitute a harmless public library with a spiteful one.
- **Hardware Attacks:** These target specific hardware components, such as webcams, keyboards, routers, etc. Usually, backdoors are inserted into hardware to carry out many of these assaults.
- **Firmware Attacks:** These occur when a virus is included into a device's boot code. When the computer boots up, this kind of

virus activates, putting the system as a whole at risk. Firmware attacks are very risky, fast, and frequently go unreported unless specially protected against.

The Persistent Vulnerability of Software Vendors

The poor security standards that penetration testing experts discover in many businesses frequently astound them. In the course of their employment, ethical hackers usually acquire total control of systems such as servers that handle updates, GitLab for version control, and those used to create programs and store digital artifacts. This degree of access shows how simple it would be for an attacker to alter these places in order to inject their own malicious code.

The safety and security of their consumers ' goods of their consumers must be the primary concern of responsible software developers. Unfortunately, it is all too usual to come across developers who lack the requisite cybersecurity expertise. Software producers still have serious vulnerabilities to security threats, despite the fact that they frequently take precautions to protect their products.

In these situations, the compromised vendor unintentionally sends its clients tainted code, libraries, or updates, which gives an attacker access to the clients' IT systems. After gaining access, a hacker may stealthily steal information, cause havoc, or generate a virus. This malware can later be spread via the network to important systems like customer databases or financial servers. The organization will be under a great threat of data loss unless it has a good backup strategy.

Common Internal Supply Chain Vulnerabilities

- **Inadequate Inventory Management**

  This could result in called inventory shortage or surplus inventory generated by poor inventory management that's exposing your supply chain to vulnerability. Inadequate stock could lead to loss of sales and unhappy customers, whereas surplus inventory causes the blockage of capital and more expenditures on storage facilities. These vulnerabilities can be mitigated by putting in place demand forecasting tools and real-time inventory tracking systems, which can be utilized to maximize inventory levels.

- **Lack of Supply Chain Visibility and Transparency**

  However, with limited visibility of the operations of your supply chain, you find it difficult to locate the bottlenecks, monitor shipments efficiently and predict the problems before it turns into an issue. This weakness is especially pronounced in the multi-layer supply chains that are complex and could have siloed or lagging information.

  Without a high-level supply chain visibility, companies tend to have difficulties with:

  - Monitor inventory correctly in locations.
  - Keep track of supplier performance and compliance.
  - Predict possible upheavals, in advance of their effects.
  - Make sound decisions in real-time.

- **Supplier Dependency and Lack of Redundancy**

  The use of one supplier or a few suppliers of the essential parts provides a high vulnerability. Should that supplier have issues, then the whole operation may not work. The strong supply chain needs to have strategic redundancy; that is, the presence of alternative suppliers and alternative plans that can be used in cases where the primary sources are inaccessible.

- **Poor or Age-Old Processes.**

  Inefficiencies caused by manual procedures, paper-based systems, and outdated workflows are likely to exacerbate the effects of disruptions. Your supply chain is more vulnerable to both internal and external factors since these processes are typically slower, less flexible, and more imprecise than the digital alternatives.

- **Risks of technology and system downtime.**

  Poor or non-relevant technology infrastructure may result in cyber threats, data breaches and downtimes. Technology could be used to strengthen the supply chain but it could be exploited by a security threat should it not be maintained and ensured. There is a necessity to mitigate these technology-related vulnerabilities by means of regular system maintenance, updates, and backup processes.

- **Human Error and Skills Gaps**

  Lack of training, human error, and lack of knowledge among employees on practices involving the supply chain can pose a major vulnerability. Common issues include:

  - Lack of proper training on the important systems and processes.
  - Lack of skills in major areas of operation.
  - Lack of standard use of procedures and protocols.
  - Team or interdepartmental breakdowns in communications.

  These vulnerabilities can be addressed by investing in extensive training courses and transparent standard operating procedures.

- **Legal Risks and regulatory compliance.**

  The legal consequences of not adhering to the applicable rules and laws are a potential lawsuit and a bad image. Multi-country supply chains are faced with specific issues of going through various regulatory environments, which may be conflicting. These legal weaknesses should be addressed by ensuring that strong compliance monitoring and management systems are put in place.

- **Change Management Challenges**

  The adoption of new organizational structures, procedures, or systems without proper change management may bring with it temporary but major vulnerability. Otherwise, positive changes to your supply chain operations can be sabotaged by resistance to change, insufficient training, and ineffective implementation planning.

Common External Supply Chain Vulnerabilities

- **Market Volatility and Economic Fluctuations**

  Costs and material availability are impacted by market demand, commodity prices, and exchange rate variations. These factors can disrupt supply chains by affecting customer demand, cost, and material availability. The worldwide supply chain of the companies makes them especially vulnerable to economic unpredictability in various areas. These vulnerabilities can be alleviated by ensuring that the economic scenario planning is developed and that financial flexibility is maintained.

- **Logisticd Transportation Disruptions.**

  The infrastructure, regulation, or natural disaster delays and interruptions in transportation can have a devastating effect on the supply chain operations. Interlocution movement of goods is a very crucial weakness of most supply chains. Disruptions resulting in transportation may be caused by:

  - Congestion or malfunctions in the infrastructure
  - Limitations on carrier capacity
  - The unpredictability of fuel prices
  - Strikes and labor disputes
  - Customs problems and border delays
  - Breakdowns of vehicles or vessels

  These vulnerabilities can be managed by deploying real-time tracking systems and diversifying carriers and routes of transportation.

- **Geopolitical and Trade-Related Risks**

  The factors that hinder the global supply chain operations include political instability, trade disputes, and sanctions. These can cause a rise in costs, delays or even block the entry of some markets or suppliers altogether. Internationally-based companies need to keep an eye on the geopolitical situation and devise backup strategies in case of a disaster in the targeted regions.

- **Natural Disasters and Natural Environmental Events.**

  The harsh disruptions caused by earthquakes, hurricanes, floods, and other natural disasters in susceptible areas may destroy infrastructure, interrupt the transport systems, and impact facilities for production. The frequency and severity of these occurrences are increasing due to climate change, posing the supply chains in the world with an increasing vulnerability. The mitigation strategies necessary include geographic diversification and a strong disaster recovery plan.

- **Data Breaches and Cybersecurity Threats.**

  Cyber-attacks can interfere with vital operations and sensitive information by causing data breaches and theft of intellectual property as well as disruption of operations. According to the state of supply chain defense report by Blue Voyant, supply chain cybersecurity breaches per company in 2023 is 4.16, higher than in 2022 of 3.29. The interconnectedness of the contemporary supply chains implies that any weakness within the systems of one organization has the potential to impact most of the rest of the organizations within the network.

To minimize vulnerabilities, it is important to implement thorough maritime cybersecurity across your supply chain. Organizations should target protection techniques that safeguard the information system and operational technologies that support the important supply chain operations.

20. INCIDENT RESPONSE AND CONTINUITY PLANNING

Cybersecurity incident response and continuity planning are intended to make organizations prevent cyber threats, such as cyberattacks, computer data breaches, ransomware, and system intrusions. The procedure of responding to an incident is identifying, analyzing, and managing security events in a way that is likely to prevent maximum harm and recover systems within the shortest time. In the modern world of strong interconnection, it is crucial to have an organized mechanism of response to curb the effects of cyber events on sensitive data and major operations.

A cybersecurity incident response plan is normally Preparation, detection, analysis, containment, eradication, and recovery are all part of an organized lifecycle. In the case of an attack, security personnel strive to find the origin and nature of the threat as quickly as possible, bring the infected systems under isolation, and remove malicious code. Communication protocols and documentation are also part of effective incident response, and all stakeholders need to be notified, and lessons learned can be used to consolidate future protection.

Cyber continuity planning allows organizations to ensure that they will not lose their necessary digital services and business operations even if there is a cyber incident. This entails the provision of backup systems, disaster recovery infrastructures and redundancy of infrastructure to ensure availability. As an example, companies can rely on cloud-based backup systems, loading mechanisms, and information replication plans so that important information and applications are available even in case of disruption.

Incident response and continuity planning are a complete cyber resilience approach. As incident response is preoccupied with the management of threats at the moment, continuity planning guarantees the recovery in the long-term and stability in operations. A combination of the two approaches will allow the organizations to decrease downtime, safeguard sensitive data, and instill trust even in the conditions of even more sophisticated cyber-attacks.

What are security incidents

Any physical or digital breach that jeopardizes the availability, confidentiality, or integrity of an organization's information systems or sensitive data is referred to as a security incident or security event. Security incidents can include both unintentional violations of IT security standards by authorized users and deliberate cyberattacks by hackers or unauthorized users.

These are some of the most common security incidents:

- **Ransomware**

  Sometimes referred to as ransomware, Malicious software locks down a victim's computer device or data and threatens to keep it locked or worse unless the victim pays a ransom.

- **Phishing and social engineering**

  Phishing assaults are verbal or digital communications intended to trick users into disclosing personal information, downloading malicious software, sending money or assets to the wrong person, or carrying out other harmful actions.

  Phishing emails are crafted by attackers to appear or sound as though they are from a reputable company or person, sometimes even someone the receiver knows personally.

- **DDoS assaults**

  In a distributed denial-of-service (DDoS) attack, hackers take over multiple computers and use them to flood the servers or network of a target business with fictitious traffic, preventing genuine users from accessing those resources.

- **Attacks on supply chains**

  Supply chain assaults are cyberattacking that enter a target organization by focusing on its suppliers. This could entail, for example, utilizing a vendor's services to spread malware or leveraging the theft of private information from a supplier's systems.

- **Threats from within**

  Insider dangers come in two varieties. Partners, staff members, or other authorized users who purposefully jeopardize an organization's information security are known as malicious insiders. Authorized users who inadvertently jeopardize security by disregarding security best practices, such as creating weak passwords or keeping private information in dangerous locations, are known as negligent insiders.

- **Privilege escalation attacks**

  In some cases, an assailant initially obtains restricted access to a system, then leverages that access to advance laterally, obtaining higher privileges and more sensitive data in the process.

  The attacker may be able to increase their privileges or gain initial access with the aid of stolen credentials.

Incident response planning

An organization's attempts to manage incidents are usually guided by an incident response strategy. Plans are frequently created and carried out by a "computer security incident response team" (CSIRT) made up of stakeholders from around the organization.

The CSIRT team may include IT staff, security analysts, the "chief information security officer" (CISO), and the "security operations center" (SOC). There may also be representation from executive leadership, legal, human resources, risk management, regulatory compliance, and maybe third-party experts from service providers.

"By investing in response preparedness, organizations can help reduce the costly, disruptive effects of data breaches, support operational continuity, and help preserve their relationships with customers, partners, and other key stakeholders," according to the Report on the Cost of a Data Breach.

Typically, an incident response plan consists of:

- An incident response playbook that outlines each CSIRT member's duties and responsibilities over the course of the incident response lifecycle.
- The technology installed throughout the organization, including software, hardware, and security measures.
- A business continuity plan that outlines how to quickly restore critical systems and data in the case of an outage.

- A method for handling incidents that specifies exactly what needs to be done at each step of the procedure and by whom.
- A plan for communicating events to clients, staff, management, and law enforcement.
- Instructions for gathering and recording incident data for postmortem examination and, if required, court cases.

Since each sort of occurrence may call for a different reaction, the CSIRT may create distinct incident response plans for each. For ransomware, malware, phishing, DDoS assaults, and insider threats, many organizations have dedicated incident response strategies.

To reduce the time it takes to respond, correct, and recover from an attack, incident response tactics tailored to an organization's environment or environments are required.

To supplement their internal CSIRTs, several businesses work with outside partners who provide incident response services. These collaborators often operate on a retainer basis and support the creation and implementation of incident response plans, among other areas of the broader incident management process.

How incident response works

Based on models created by the "National Institute of Standards and Technology" (NIST) 1 and SANS Institute 2, the majority of incident response plans adhere to the same general incident response framework. Typical incident response procedures consist of:

- **Preparation**

  Furthermore, incident response is still in its early stages. In order to respond, identify, contain, and recover from an event as fast as feasible while causing the least amount of disruption to business, the CSIRT chooses the appropriate protocols, instruments, and strategies.

  The business environment that has to be secured, possible network vulnerabilities, and other kinds of security incidents that could endanger the network are all identified by the CSIRT through routine risk assessment. Each kind of occurrence is ranked by the team based on how it might affect the company.

The CSIRT may "wargame" a variety of attack tactics before generating templates of the best reactions to speed action in an actual attack. To provide metrics for upcoming drills and potential assaults, response time could be monitored. The CSIRT may create new incident response plans or revise current ones based on a thorough risk assessment.

- **Detection and analysis**

The team monitors any threats and unusual network activity during this phase. To find recurring issues, they examine data, alerts, and notifications from device logs and other security technologies (firewalls, antivirus software). By categorizing the actual alerts according to severity, the team attempts to differentiate between genuine situations and false positives.

To monitor security events in real time and automate response operations, the majority of enterprises nowadays utilize one or more security systems, such as "security information and event management" (SIEM) and "endpoint detection and response" (EDR). For more information, see the "Incident response technologies" section.

At this stage, the communication plan is equally crucial. The CSIRT will notify the relevant staff and proceed to the next phase of the incident response procedure after determining the type of threat or breach they are addressing.

- **Containment**

The incident response team acts to stop further damage to the network harmed by the breach or other malicious activities. After that, the emergency incident response strategies are implemented. Containment activities fall into two groups:

- By isolating the impacted systems, such as by taking infected devices offline, short-term mitigation strategies aim to stop the current threat from spreading.

- ◈ Long-term confinement strategies concentrate on safeguarding unaffected systems by enclosing them in more robust security measures, such as isolating sensitive databases from the rest of the network.
- ◈ In order to stop further data loss and gather forensic evidence of the incident for future investigation, the CSIRT may now make backups of both impacted and unaffected systems.

▲ **Eradication**

The team proceeds to comprehensive repair and removal from the system after the threat has been reduced. Malware removal and the removal of an unauthorized or rogue user from the network are two examples of this. To make sure there is no remaining proof of the compromise, the team thoroughly examines both compromised and unaffected systems.

▲ **Healing**

The incident response team restores impacted systems to regular operation once they are certain that the threat has been completely eliminated. Rebuilding systems from backups, installing fixes, and restarting devices and systems are some possible solutions. For analysis and system enhancements, a record of the attack and its resolution is kept.

▲ **Post-incident review**

The CSIRT gathers evidence of the breach and records the actions taken to contain and eliminate the threat at each stage of the incident response procedure. In order to better comprehend the event and compile "lessons learned," the CSIRT now examines this data. The CSIRT looks for the underlying cause of the assault and determines how it successfully penetrated the network, and addresses vulnerabilities in order to stop similar attacks in the future.

In order to boost incident response operations against future attacks, the CSIRT also evaluates what worked and searches for ways to enhance systems, tools, and procedures. The post-incident inquiry may also involve law enforcement, depending on the specifics of the intrusion.

Continuity Planning in the Face of Cyber Threats

The idea of continuity planning in relation to cyber threats is aimed at making sure that the important business processes can proceed normally even in case the systems are affected. With the increased reliance of an organization on digital infrastructure, cyber-attacks like ransomware attacks, distributed denial-of-service attacks, and data breaches are increasingly threatening the stability of the organization's operations. A continuity plan is well organized and it identifies key assets, prioritization of key services and predefined procedures to ensure continuity in case of a cyber incident and after the incident.

One of the major elements of continuity planning is the coordination of cybersecurity with business continuity and disaster recovery plans. This involves the introduction of redundancy, data backups, and failover to be in place in case of quick recovery. It is also required that organizations identify roles and responsibilities, which can be used to prompt an effective incident response team. Risk assessments and scenario planning would regularly assist in determining the vulnerabilities and planning the relevant mitigation measures to minimize the loss of time and money.

The other consideration is the communication and coordination in case of a cyber crisis. Continuity planning is effective as stakeholders such as the employees, customers, and even partners are notified of continuity plans via reliable and safe channels of communication. This averts misinformation, retains trust and favors the coordinated recovery activities. Training and simulations also prepare staff by training them on response measures and decision-making under stress.

Lastly, continuity planning is not a single event but a continuous process that advances with the emerging threats of cyber-attacks. Businesses are to continuously check their positions concerning security, update their strategies, and consider the experience of the past events. Through their proactive and reactive vision, the businesses will become resilient and safeguard essential business operations and have a long-term presence in an ever-antagonistic cyber world.

21. INDUSTRY IMPACT: OPERATIONAL CONTINUITY AND RESILIENCE

In the modern globalized society, social and business organizations cannot exist without digital systems to be used effectively. However, malware, phishing, and ransomware are starting to pose a serious threat to these systems. Such attacks can have disastrous consequences, including commercial disruption. processes, theft of valuable information, and huge financial and reputational losses. Whether a cyberattack will take place or when no longer remains a question, but it will happen.

Cyber resilience not only serves to prevent attacks, but also to be able to respond and recover to attacks. It includes the development of flexible systems in the event of disruption and their speedy recovery of regular functions with minimum effects on operations. It could be an outbreak of ransomware, a data breach or the failure of its infrastructure, but through resilience, a strong organization is capable of adapting, recovering and getting back on its feet within the shortest time.

Cyber resilience, in short, offers a more comprehensive and strategic view that integrates excellent cybersecurity controls with a well-established business continuity and disaster recovery planning. Such a holistic strategy will guarantee that the organizations are able to not only repel the attacks but also recover fast whenever disruptions strike as it happens.

Core Components of Cyber Resilience

Cyber resilience entails the development of a strong and dynamic structure, which is resistant to cyber threats and ensures the continuity of critical functions. The major elements that can be considered in a total cyber resiliency plan are:

Cybersecurity: Protecting Data at Its Core

Data security is the most precious asset of any organization, and it is the foundation of cyber resiliency. It is crucial to concentrate on data security in order to prevent unauthorized access, ensure confidentiality, and maintain data integrity. Important components consist of:

- **Data Encryption:** When delicate data is encrypted, and it is lost, it is lost in encrypted form and even intercepted data would be useless and would be in an encrypted form.
- **Control over Access and Authentication**: "Multi-factor authentication" (MFA), "role-based access control" (RBAC), and "privileged access management" (PAM) should be used to only grant access to authorized users of vital information and systems.
- **Data Immutability:** Making use of technology like "write-once, read-many" (WORM) storage to ensure that data cannot be altered or removed once it has been written. Immutability can be very helpful in protecting against malicious software like ransomware interference.
- **Data Validity Checks**: Data integrity checks e.g. cryptographic hash can be implemented to guarantee that the data has not been corrupted or changed in any way when it was stored or transferred.
- **Continuous Monitoring and Auditing:** It is a form of tracking behaviour patterns and real-time data access to identify irregularities and conducting regular audits to ensure that the protocols of security are being followed and that opportunities to exploit vulnerabilities are detected.

With these areas in mind, the organizations are able to guard their data and reduce the chances of breaches or tampering and thus establish a robust defensive basis.

Business Continuity: High Availability and Failover Mechanisms

Business continuity covers the ability to continue with the most important operations despite a cyber incident or a system failure. High availability and smooth recovery mechanisms should be of great concern to organizations so that a disruption is minimized. The core elements include:

- **High Availability:** Designing schemes to maintain constant availability of the vital services. This will entail creating schemes that are capable of auto recovery in case of failures with the least time.
- **Multi-Way Data Replication:** This is the replication of data in more than two places that are located at different geographical points. Even in the case one of the places fails, the rest of the places will still be able to give accurate and up-to-date information, and service will not stop.

The following are Failover, Resynchronization and Failback:

- **Failover:** When a system fails, there is an automatic transfer of the operations to a backup system or redundancy system, and operations are not affected.
- **Resynchronization:** After the primary system is brought back online, the data and systems are resynchronized to make sure that there are no differences between the restored system and the backup.
- **Failback:** Operations can revert to the primary system following resynchronization without sacrificing data or service quality.

With such strategies, business continuity will guarantee that the main operations are not affected, and chiefly, the disruption is limited even during the failure of the system or attacks.

Incident Response: Rapid Detection and Containment

Even with the best precautions, incidents sometimes occur. A company can more readily identify, contain, and lessen the impact of cyber threats with the use of an effective incident response plan. Important elements consist of:

- **Threat Detection:** With the help of "Security Information and Event Management" (SIEM) platforms, "intrusion detection systems" (IDS), and Real-time behavioral analytics, anomalous activity can be detected, and early intervention can be performed.

- **Immediate Containment**: When the threat has been identified, quick containment measures, e.g., isolating breached systems, are used to contain the spread of the attack through the network.
- **Communication Protocols**: It is essential to create open lines of communication with the important internal and external stakeholders so that they take timely action. This involves reporting to leaders, IT, customers and the regulatory authorities where necessary.

An effective response plan will reduce the impact and achieve a better recovery process to avoid compromising the operational integrity and customer confidence.

Key Threats to Cyber Resilience

There are numerous threats to cyber resilience that are always presented by malicious actors as well as internal vulnerabilities. The following are the major threats that should be handled by organizations to guarantee continued resilience:

1. **Cyberattacks**

   Cyberattacks are increasingly widespread and complex. The most prevalent forms of attacks are:

   - **Malware:** Viruses, trojans and worms are malicious code that infects systems and destroys them.
   - **Phishing:** Bad actors work to deceive people into revealing personal information, including logins and other sensitive data.
   - **Ransomware:** Hackers encrypt the data and then require a ransom fee to release the encrypted data of a victim, threatening to destroy a lot of data or cause the downfall of a system.

- **Distributed Denial of Service (DDoS):** Flooding of a website or facility with volume traffic, making it inaccessible to honest users.

2. **Human Error**

Not every threat is of a menacing nature. Cyber resiliency can also be under threat of human error. Inadvertently, employees may breach security by:

- Falling victim to phishing schemes.
- Misconfiguring systems.
- Reusing passwords on many platforms or using weak passwords. To reduce these risks, it is essential to make sure staff members receive cybersecurity best practices training.

3. **System Failures**

Despite the presence of a well-developed system of cybersecurity, the systems themselves might be a weak spot because they are old or simply in a bad state of condition. Failures can occur due to software weaknesses, unpatched systems or due to the absence of redundancy of vital systems that interfere with business processes. These failures can be prevented by regular updates of the system and infrastructure audits.

4. **Natural Disasters**

Although it is not related directly Physical IT infrastructure may be destroyed by natural disasters like earthquakes, fires, or floods in addition to cyberattacks. Possessing backup systems on the geography of the data, cloud-based solutions, and disaster recovery plans are crucial towards resiliency against the occurrence of these unexpected incidents.

After being aware of these threats and how to prepare against they are the first step in building a robust company.

MULTIPLE CHOICE QUESTIONS (MCQS)

1. **What is the primary focus of Critical Infrastructure Protection (CIP)?**

   A. Enhancing social media security

   B. Protecting essential systems and assets vital to society

   C. Developing mobile applications

   D. Increasing internet speed

2. **Which of the following is considered a critical infrastructure sector?**

   A. Entertainment

   B. Agriculture

   C. Energy

   D. Tourism

3. **Why are energy systems highly targeted by cyber threats?**

   A. They store personal data

   B. They control national defense

   C. They are essential for economic and social stability

   D. They are easy to hack

4. **What is a major risk to financial systems in a hyperconnected world?**

   A. Hardware failure only

   B. Cyberattacks like ransomware and fraud

   C. Lack of employees

   D. Power shortages

5. **In healthcare systems, cyberattacks can directly impact:**
   A. Entertainment services
   B. Patient safety and medical operations
   C. Marketing strategies
   D. Weather forecasting
6. **What does SCADA stand for?**
   A. Secure Control and Data Analysis
   B. Supervisory Control and Data Acquisition
   C. System Control and Data Access
   D. Standard Communication and Data Application
7. **Industrial Control Systems (ICS) are mainly used for:**
   A. Social networking
   B. Managing industrial processes and operations
   C. Online shopping
   D. Email communication
8. **Supply chain vulnerabilities arise due to:**
   A. Strong encryption
   B. Interdependence among multiple vendors and systems
   C. Lack of internet
   D. Reduced globalization
9. **What is the primary goal of incident response planning?**
   A. Prevent all cyberattacks completely
   B. Eliminate employees
   C. Detect, respond to, and recover from incidents effectively
   D. Increase profits

10. **Continuity planning ensures:**
    A. Business stops during incidents
    B. Systems are permanently shut down
    C. Operations continue during and after disruptions
    D. Only data backup is maintained

Answers

1	2	3	4	5	6	7	8	9	10
B	C	C	B	B	B	B	B	C	C

Chapter 4

AI-DRIVEN THREAT DETECTION AND INTELLIGENT DEFENSE SYSTEMS

22. OVERVIEW

The rapid evolution of digital technologies, systems that are interconnected and ecosystems that are data-driven has transformed the nature of cyber threats significantly. As stated above, cyber risk is no longer confined to a particular system, but it is now going to scale-global supply chains, national infrastructure and critical industries. The old methods of cybersecurity based on fixed rules, signature-based detection and manual intervention are becoming ineffective in this dynamic threat environment. The current cyber attackers are very sophisticated, automated and adaptive; they will get around the traditional defenses, and it is necessary to be smarter and more proactive with the security mechanisms (Shrivastav, 2025).

Artificial Intelligence has revolutionized the world of cybersecurity by enabling businesses to recognize, evaluate, and respond to threats more quickly and precisely than ever before. With the help of high volumes of data that are collected on networks, devices, and interactions between users, AI-driven systems become capable of identifying patterns, understanding anomalies, and anticipating possible attacks before they become real. In contrast to conventional systems, AI-based systems continuously adapt to new information and, therefore, respond to changes in threat behavior, as well as minimize the time taken to detect and eliminate risks.

In this chapter, the author discusses how AI is used to continuously progress threat discovery and develop intelligent defense systems, which can operate in a complex and large-scale environment. It starts by reviewing the application of machine learning methods in cybersecurity, in which the various learning paradigms can be used to identify and classify threats. The next discussion is the behavioral analytics and anomaly detection, which dwells on detecting abnormal system and user behavior to detect obscured or emergent threats.

Also, using Security Orchestration, Automation, and Response (SOAR) systems, the chapter explores the growing significance of automation in cybersecurity operations. The systems allow quicker and more coordinated reactions to the incidents and decrease the manualization of the processes, enhancing the overall efficiency of the work. Another way the chapter explores the use of AI to identify and neutralize advanced persistent threats (APTs) is that they are highly covert and long-lasting attacks that are commonly related to state actors (Barakat, 2025).

Besides the advantages, this chapter critically looks at the ethical and security issues that are involved in the application of AI in cyber defense. To present a balanced picture, issues such as the presence of algorithmic bias, adversarial attacks, data privacy, and the dual-use characteristic of AI technologies are touched upon. Finally, the chapter critically evaluates the broader industry-wide implications of AI-based cybersecurity, especially the impact of AI-based cybersecurity on operational resiliency, risk management and the future of digital defense strategies.

All in all, AI is becoming the primary pillar in the advancement of the new cybersecurity since it would enable the shift towards proactive, intelligent and scalable security mechanisms, which would be able to react to the cyber threat at scale.

23. MACHINE LEARNING IN CYBERSECURITY

Machine learning in cybersecurity refers to the use of data-driven algorithms to automatically learn and respond to online threats and prevent them. ML models look at the patterns of network traffic, user behaviour and system logs in order to locate anomalies that could indicate cyberattacks, instead of relying only on a set of previously established parameters. This intelligent automation makes it possible to detect faster, reduce false alarms and provide a more robust defense against dynamic threats, which the more traditional security techniques often fail to detect.

Besides enhancing threat detection, machine learning is never the same since it continually acquires new data. Cybersecurity systems can anticipate new attack paths before the latter can even inflict any damage due to their flexibility. ML can empower security personnel to move beyond reactiveness in defense to proactive threat prevention by uncovering latent patterns and correlating huge amounts of information on the fly. This will increase resilience and reduce the risk timeframe across digital ecosystems.

Uses of Machine Learning in Cybersecurity

These are primary applications of Machine Learning to Cybersecurity:

1. **Early Threat Detection**

   - **Detection of the Malware and Phishing Attempts:** Machine learning is also good at detecting malicious files, links, and emails by using the patterns that are out of the ordinary. A more traditional signature-based system does not respond to the changing threats, such as those that apply more advanced obfuscation methods, in contrast to ML. Organizations can stay ahead of the attackers and improve the rate of early detection with real-time flexibility.

   - **Detecting Unusual Network Traffic:** Machine learning algorithms can analyze massive amounts of network data to detect suspicious behaviour, which may signal the start of a cyberattack, including unusual data transfer or unusual login attempts. These data can be automatically processed to minimize the time of response and accelerate the detection of potential threats.

2. **Incident Response**

   ◈ **Automated Security Actions:** ML-powered systems are capable of automatically and immediately responding to a breach, including locking down vulnerable accounts, preventing suspicious IP addresses or isolating infected devices without requiring human interaction. This level of automation accelerates reaction times as security teams are able to focus on difficult tasks that require human capability.

   ◈ **Quicker, More Exact Threat Neutralization:** ML processing and data examination can give security staff the opportunity to counteract assaults in a manner that is both timely and effective. This speed reduces the chances of human error and potential damage. Threat mitigation activities are also enhanced by better data contextualization to improve their accuracy.

3. **Reducing Costs**

   ◈ Machine learning reduces the manual load of processes such as vulnerability checks and log analysis. Consequently, organizations can invest in other important elements of their cybersecurity infrastructures. Machine learning enhances productivity across the entire security operations by automating repetitive workflows and simplifying the work process.

Types of Machine Learning in Cybersecurity

The different ML approaches that are used to respond to different cybersecurity requirements mean that organizations can deploy tailor-made solutions to threat detection and response.

1. **Learning of Rule-Based Automation:** Supervised learning involves the use of labeled datasets that the algorithms are

trained on to detect a specific type of hazard. An example is that it can recognize the known malware types or phishing emails and even trigger automatic operations, including reaching out to the relevant teams or isolating susceptible systems.

2. **Unsupervised Learning of Anomaly Detection:** In contrast to supervised learning, unsupervised learning detects unknown patterns in unlabeled data by analyzing them. It can be used especially well to identify outliers in security logs or to identify suspicious activity in network traffic, which could be a sign of a zero-day attack or an insider threat.

3. **Dynamical Adaptive Threat Response Reinforcement Learning:** Reinforcement learning allows for improving machine learning models and learning through interaction with the environment. Depending on the success of the previous activities, these models, among others, can streamline defense systems, e.g., changing firewall settings or intrusion prevention systems settings.

Benefits of Machine Learning in Cybersecurity

1. **Improved Accuracy in Threat Detection:** The declining probability of missed threats is attributed to the fact that ML models can identify suspicious activities more precisely than traditional methods due to the analysis of massive datasets.

2. **Real-time Analysis and Response Capabilities:** ML-driven systems process the information in real-time, which enables businesses to reduce the potential damage by identifying and preventing threats as they occur.

3. **False Positives and Negatives Reduction:** As time goes on, machine learning keeps on advancing its algorithms and thus generates a reduced number of inaccurate alarms. This can ensure that security teams focus on actual issues instead of wasting their resources on an unwarranted task.

4. **Scalability in Processing Large Data Volume: ML scales well to examine the growing volume of data generated by**

organizations, users, devices, and applications to provide security in large and complex infrastructures.

Examples of Machine Learning in Cybersecurity Tools

- **Anti-virus and anti-malware:** Classify and detect malicious software such as zero-day threats and classify them based on code characteristics, behaviour, or execution patterns using machine learning.
- **Cloud security posture management (CSPM):** Machine learning enhances CSPM solutions by identifying configuration errors, abnormal behavior in the cloud environment, and possible policy violations, according to usage patterns.
- **Gateways for email security:** Apply machine learning to content, sender behaviour, and URL trends to identify phishing, spoofing, and business email compromise.
- **Endpoint detection and response (EDR):** Behavioral anomalies can be detected, and machine learning can be used to track and analyze endpoint activity and detect threats instead of using attack signatures alone.
- **Systems for detecting and preventing intrusions (IDPS):** Even in situations when attack signatures are unknown, use machine learning to identify unusual network traffic patterns and stop illegal access.
- **Analysis of network traffic:** To detect lateral movement, data exfiltration, and command-and-control communication, use machine learning to examine network traffic data for anomalies.
- **Information and event management for security (SIEM):** Use machine learning to reduce false positives, discover anomalies, and correlate events based on past security event data.
- **Security orchestration, automation, and response (SOAR):** According to threat intelligence and behavioral analysis, use machine learning to rank and recommend or automate response actions on alerts.

- **Analytics of user and entity behaviour (UEBA):** Learn standards of normal user and system behaviour with machine learning and detect any non-standard behaviour, which may indicate a threat of malefactors among insiders or external threat agents.

24. EHAVIORAL ANALYTICS AND ANOMALY DETECTION

Behavior anomaly detection refers to the finding of abnormal patterns in data. These trends can be referred to as anomalies, outliers or exceptions, which may indicate severe issues such as system malfunctions or security violations.

Algorithmsanalyzeextensivedatavolumesanddistinguishbetween ordinary patterns and abnormal ones, aiding in the recognition of any threat or malfunction at the initial stage. Machine learning, statistical measures, and near-real-time analytics are used to detect anomalies in order to identify discrepancies. It is applied in numerous other areas, with cybersecurity as the most significant, where abnormalities can be signs of invasions or breaches.

Types of Anomalies

These are the main forms of anomalies that anomaly detection systems tend to analyze.

1. **Point Deviations**

   In case the difference in one of the data values is significant compared to other data, it is referred to as a point anomaly. These are the points that are typically distant in a normal distribution, implying the deviations that could indicate errors or abnormal activity. In these processes, like fraud detection, where a single aberrant transaction can be evidence of unauthorized actions, it is necessary to identify point anomalies.

   These anomalies are often detected using statistical criteria or machine learning models that have been trained to detect normal behaviour of data. Detecting anomalies at the point of early occurrence assists in minimizing and preventing potential security breaches. As an example, the presence of a single suspicious transaction in the banking sector can be a sign of underlying widespread fraud patterns.

2. **Contextual Anomalies**

In certain conditions under which a point is an abnormality, the point is referred to as a contextual anomaly. These are dependent on its context and the measurements around it, unlike point anomalies, which are always deviating. An increase in network traffic, e.g., in the peak time but alarming at midnight, is normal. This detection requires the comprehension of the common settings of the dataset.

These anomalies are essential in cybersecurity situations, such as the monitoring of seasonal transactions or the monitoring of user behaviour. Systems need to consider numerous factors in order to properly identify risks and give relevant alerts without unnecessary false alarms. The use of both spatial and temporal data can help organizations to manage risks.

3. **Collective Anomalies**

A collection of data points that are not in themselves different but which form an unexpected pattern with one another is called a collective anomaly. An example of such intrusion is a distributed denial-of-service attack (DDoS), which can be recommended by several small deviations, which would not have been noticed when considered individually. Collective anomaly detection is significant in security settings that are prone to long-running, covert attacks that may be aimed at supporting a slowing down of the performance of the system without causing an immediate alert.

Collective anomaly detection in cybersecurity is used to maintain track of system health over time and detect repeated threatening activities. Algorithms examine sequences and correlations of datasets to indicate underlying patterns that may indicate potential dangers. By detecting these patterns of unusual occurrences, organizations would be better equipped to provide a defense mechanism.

Methods of Anomaly Detection

There are various ways of detecting anomalous behaviour.

1. **Statistical Methods**

   Statistical methods of aberrant detection depend on the underlying data distribution models to determine outliers. Such models are capable of detecting anomalies that may be in the form of variations by understanding statistical characteristics such as mean and variance. Common methodologies that are simple but can be used in specific circumstances include z-score, T-test and chi-square tests.

   The methods are most effective when the distribution of the data is well-defined and requires some predetermined thresholds. Despite the simplicity of statistical methods, they are not appropriate to deal with complex data patterns and modern cybersecurity threats. Their use in the real world is often restricted because they make assumptions about data distribution, especially when the data is dynamic and heterogeneous.

2. **Rule-Based Methods**

   Early SIEMs were based on rule-based anomaly detection, which meant that anomalies were detected based on pre-established rules and patterns. These rules are typically based on standardized if-else based rules that security teams have devised to detect items of data that do not behave as they should. This approach is also useful in an environment where the abnormalities have distinct patterns because it offers urgency and predictability.

   Rule-based approaches have scalability and adaptability issues, though, in the case of dynamic environments where attack strategies are continuously evolving. They often cause a large number of false positives or false negatives when the enemies avoid using fixed detection logic, as they require constant tuning and maintenance. Cyber threats are becoming sophisticated and rule-based systems alone cannot be used to detect subtle, unknown, or low-and-slow attacks.

3. **Cluster-Based Methods**

   Data points in cluster-based anomaly detection would be clustered, and any data that greatly goes out of these clusters would be spotted. The clusters are created dynamically depending on similarity using algorithms such as the k-means or the DBSCAN, which consider the non-reliable points as an aberration. Multi-dimensional data are also suitable for these techniques, as it is possible to identify outliers based on the interactions among the variables.

   Because clusters that are misidentified may result in abnormalities being missed, cluster-based methods are only effective when they are able to represent data in the right way. Regular operations, which are relatively stable, come in handy when it comes to cybersecurity in identifying patterns of unusual behaviour.

4. **Deep Learning Approaches**

   Deep learning methods also improve the detection of anomalies as they can analyze large and complex data. Artificial neural networks used in these techniques include convolutional and recurrent neural networks, which are used to extract features and identify anomalies. They particularly perform well in those cases when unstructured data is abundant.

   The efficacy of deep learning methods is despite the fact that they consume a lot of resources and demand a lot of processing power to train and deploy. They provide a significant contribution to cybersecurity by providing higher detection rates of intricate anomalies in large and diverse data.

Challenges in Anomaly Detection

The following are some of the key issues that may complicate the process of identifying anomalies.

1. **Data Quality Issues**

   Due to the possibility of wrong interpretation with poor or incorrect data, data quality is a significant hindrance to anomaly detection. Poor data quality can result in distortion of results, the generation of noise or unnoticed anomalies. This is typical of cybersecurity, where data are received at different and heterogeneous sources, often asynchronously, to introduce flaws and noise that complicate the detection of anomalies.

2. **High False Positives**

   False positives are high when the normal operations are falsely reported as abnormalities, and this overwhelms the security personnel with excessive alarms. This can lead to alert weariness that reduces the reaction time and increases the chances of not detecting real threats. A behavior-based approach, such as User and Entity Behaviour Analytics (UEBA), can be used to reduce false positives by assessing activity based on the previous behaviour and peer-group comparisons. UEBA is associated with numerous signals, learns dynamically to the evolving patterns, and offers the risk rating to anomalies as opposed to relying on fixed thresholds. Organizational measures can be taken to reduce the noise and focus on the actual threats, including behavioral context and ranking warning in terms of risk.

3. **Asymmetries in Data Distributions.**

   In most cases, anomalies constitute a small percentage of a data set. With this imbalance, detection algorithms will be skewed to detect predominantly common patterns, and thus, it becomes harder to detect uncommon yet significant abnormalities. It is thus important to deal with imbalanced data in such a way as to use techniques such as oversampling anomalies or artificial creation of such data to balance their distributions.

4. **Evolving Threat Landscape**

   The level of cyberattacks is increasingly becoming advanced, and they are continually devising methods of concealing their activities from standard detection methods. Due to this fact, anomaly detection systems must adapt to changing patterns in real-time so that they can be in front of unknown threats and that they stay ahead of changes in the surroundings with minimal lag in detection accuracy. Machine learning models that are adaptive and other advanced technologies should be constantly developed and incorporated to identify anomalies.

Applications of Anomaly Detection in Cybersecurity

Anomaly detection technologies can be used to find different types of abnormalities.

1. **Detection of intrusions**

   Intrusion detection systems (IDS) identify activities that are not the norm, which are a pointer of potential intrusions. IDSs utilize the concept of anomaly detection to maintain a vigilant eye on the activity of users, network traffic, and system performance. They inform operators about any unusual deviations that may suggest attempts at unauthorized access.

   Also, the IDSs provide contextual alerts that provide the security teams with the information required to immediately investigate and take necessary measures. This skill is required so as to reduce the dwell time and prevent successful breaches.

2. **Fraud Detection**

   Anomaly detection is a technique of detecting fraud in any financial industry by identifying abnormal transactions that may indicate the possibility of fraud. Financial institutions such as banks can stop malicious transactions and protect the assets of consumers by detecting anomalies such as abnormal spending habits, location differences, or abnormal transaction volumes.

To ensure effective rates of sophistication, fraud prevention anomaly-detecting algorithms are based on both time and context data. To remain effective, the fraud detection systems should always be updated with the new plans and strategies of fraud. They make fraud detection more accurate by applying processing algorithms to search for complex patterns.

3. **Insider Threat Detection**

The insider threat detection involves monitoring and assessment of the behaviour of employees to detect any anomalies that would lead to a malevolent motive within the firm. Abnormal data access, unusual times of login and illegal data transfer are some of the anomalies that can indicate insider risks. By focusing on behaviour, and not on identification, anomaly detection can help to detect potential internal threats even when the attacker is a trusted insider.

As a way of resisting insider threats, detection systems should balance their privacy and security to be able to detect potential hazards and to reduce any effect on the legal operations of the entities. They are forced to continually learn and adapt baselines so that they adapt to changing behavioral patterns.

4. **Network Performance Monitoring.**

Anomaly detection in network performance monitoring is the detection of anomalies in network traffic that may indicate issues such as hardware failures, bandwidth overload or intrusion. The network performance can be maintained to optimum levels, which ensures smooth operations, through detection of irregularities like sudden bandwidth reduction or unexpected traffic bursts.

Anomaly detection systems are essential in predicting potential issues within the network prior to their impact on the performance of the network. The network performance monitoring would be ineffective without real-time anomaly detection since corrective actions would be taken quickly in order to minimize downtime and prevent inconveniences to the users.

25. AUTOMATED INCIDENT RESPONSE AND SOAR PLATFORMS

AI-powered incident response employs the use of such technologies as data analytics and machine learning to detect and fix cyber threats. The AI runs through hundreds of security alarms and measures the ones that should be addressed right now. It also begins to solve the problems without requiring human interference. This not only saves precious time but also lets security teams focus on more advanced issues that require human evaluation. Consequently, they identify and block threats much more quickly and diminish the likelihood of severe damage to the organization (Farzaan et al., 2025).

Security teams may integrate and coordinate various security solutions, automate tedious operations, and optimize incident and threat response workflows with the help of SOAR, which stands for security orchestration, automation, and response.

Security operations centers (SOCs) in large organizations use a variety of tools to monitor and react to cyber threats, frequently by hand. Overall, threat reaction times are slowed down as a result of this manual threat investigation.

SOCs can incorporate these tools into optimized threat response workflows and automate repetitive, low-level operations in those workflows by using the central console provided by SOAR platforms. Additionally, this console enables SOCs to handle all of the security warnings produced by these products in one convenient location.

Security orchestration

"Security orchestration" describes how SOAR platforms link and manage the software and hardware components of an organization's security system.

SOCs employ a variety of tools, such as firewalls, threat intelligence feeds, and endpoint protection products, to monitor and address threats. Multiple tools can be used in even basic security procedures. For instance, in order to recognize, comprehend, and eliminate the threat, a security analyst looking into a phishing email might require a secure email gateway, a threat intelligence platform, and antivirus software. Analysts must manually switch between these tools as they work because they frequently come from various suppliers and might not interact well.

SOCs can integrate these capabilities into logical, repeatable security operations (SecOps) workflows by using a SOAR. Application programming interfaces (APIs), pre-made plugins, and bespoke integrations are used by SOARs to link security (and some non-security) tools. After these technologies are linked, SOCs can use playbooks to plan their actions.

The steps of common security procedures, such as threat detection, investigation, and response, can be outlined by security analysts using playbooks, which are process maps. Playbooks can include a variety of tools and applications. They may be entirely automated, entirely manual, or a mix of both.

Security Automation

Low-level, time-consuming, repetitive processes like opening and closing support tickets, event enrichment, and alert prioritization can be automated with SOAR security solutions. Also, SOARs can activate automated actions of integrated security technologies. This means that security analysts are able to automate more complex security processes by linking a number of tools via playbook workflows.

Consider how a laptop penetration investigation may be automated using a SOAR platform, e.g., the earliest indicator that something has gone wrong is an endpoint detection and response (EDR) system that identifies the presence of suspicious activity on the laptop. The SOAR will play a pre-defined playbook once notified by the EDR. The SOAR opens an incident ticket first. Information in incorporated threat intelligence streams and other security tools is combined with the alarm to make it better. Subsequently, the SOAR is used to perform automated responses; it can be configured to trigger an endpoint quarantine via a network detection and response (NDR) tool or to instruct antivirus software to detect and delete malware. The ticket is sent to a security analyst of the SOAR, who will determine the need to involve human intervention or if the resolution has been made.

The use of artificial intelligence and machine learning can be considered one of the examples of SOARs that consider the data provided by security technologies and propose upcoming threat management plans.

Incident response

Due to its orchestration capabilities and auto-piloting, SOAR can serve as a central dashboard to security incident response (IR). According to IBM's Cost of a Data Breach research, companies that had both an IR team and IR plan testing discovered breaches 54 days sooner than those that didn't.

SOARs allow security analysts to look into and fix issues without switching between different tools. SOARs compile metrics and warnings from external feeds and integrated security systems into a consolidated dashboard, much like threat intelligence platforms. Analysts are able to prioritize alerts, filter out false positives, correlate data from various sources, and pinpoint the precise threats they are facing. Analysts can then react by initiating the relevant playbooks.

SOAR tools can also be used by SOCs for more proactive security procedures and post-incident audits. Security teams can learn how a specific threat entered the network and how to stop such threats in the future by using SOAR dashboards. Similarly, security teams can use SOAR data to pinpoint persistent, undetected risks and concentrate their threat hunting efforts in the appropriate areas.

Advantages of Automated Incident Response

AI boosts incident response with faster, smarter decisions. It offers more than simple automation by learning and adapting in real time. When you adopt AI in Incident response, your business gets numerous benefits.

1. **Rapid Detection and Response:** AI reduces the number of days or hours how long it takes to identify and address incidents to seconds or minutes. Rapid response limits damage due to violations and decreases the recovery time by a significant factor.

2. **Reduced Analyst Fatigue:** Security teams receive an unmanageable amount of alerts they receive daily. The AI filters out false positives and puts similar alerts in actionable cases. This enables the analysts to concentrate on the high-priority threats, which increase productivity and morale.

3. **24/7 Monitoring:** AI does not need breaks, holidays, or downtime. It has all-around-the-clock vigilance throughout the network, and it provides real-time protection.

4. **Scalability:** The larger the organization, the larger the cybersecurity needs are. AI is easily scalable to meet increasing amounts of data and complexity, which is why it is an appropriate choice when a company is experiencing fluctuations in its infrastructure.

5. **Predictive Capabilities:** Machine learning algorithms will be able to predict future historical attacks by observing trends and patterns in data. It allows preventive defensive measures that minimize exposure to risks.

6. **Cost-Efficiency:** The AI Incident Response saves on operational expenses by saving time and making routine work automated. It not only assists organizations to do more with less but also makes their cybersecurity program more viable.

Challenges and Limitations of SOAR

As much as Security Orchestration, Automation, and Response (SOAR) platforms offer considerable benefits in the current cybersecurity activities, their implementation and performance are linked with various challenges that organizations should put into serious consideration.

One of the outstanding challenges is the difficulty in integrating. The SOAR platforms, which may be acquired by various suppliers, require connecting to a variety of security technologies and systems that may complicate deployment and slow the efficiency of operations. Also, organizations might have challenges in integrating SOAR within their wider cybersecurity plan, especially where their current level of security maturity is not clearly established.

The second weakness that should not be ignored is the dependence on predetermined playbooks and workflows. These structured rules play an essential role in SOAR systems to make responses automatic. Nonetheless, this strictness may contribute to their weakness in the context of new or advanced threats that are not reminiscent of the established patterns.

Organizational factors are also very essential. Insufficient security culture may cause information silos and ineffective cooperation between teams and constrain the outcomes of SOAR implementations. Moreover, human expertise is frequently underestimated, and it is believed that automation can entirely substitute the analysts. As a matter of fact, human judgment is still required when dealing with complex and ambivalent security events.

Other organizations might form unrealistic expectations of the SOAR capabilities and expect the full independence of intelligence. This may be disappointing when systems perform worse than they are set to perform. In the same way, measures of success might not be clear, which may complicate quantifying the deployment of SOAR efficacy and the payback.

The second obstacle is the misunderstanding associated with SOAR that it is the same as artificial intelligence. SOAR may use AI and machine learning elements, but unless such technologies are added, it is not an intelligent system.

Even with these shortcomings, SOAR still develops and is a useful part of the current cybersecurity designs. As machine learning and artificial intelligence evolve, it is possible that the SOAR systems of the future will be more adaptable, intelligent, and have the ability to mitigate more sophisticated cyber threats.

26. AI AGAINST ADVANCED PERSISTENT THREATS (APTS)

An advanced persistent threat (APT), a highly developed and persistent cyberattack by a well-resourced adversary, typically a nation-state or state-sponsored entity, is when unauthorized access to a network is gained by an actor and remains undetected over a lengthy period of time, with the aim of stealing data, conducting espionage, or engaging in sabotage activities (Ali et al., 2025).

The NIST Computer Security Resource Center defines an APT as an adversary that has advanced capabilities of knowledge and substantial resources that make it feasible to establish avenues to accomplishment on its goals through the application of more than one attack vector. These three characteristics of APTs in comparison with conventional cyberattacks are summarized by this formal definition.

Advanced. Custom malware, zero-day exploits and advanced evasion methods are among the APT threat actors. They change their tooling in the middle of the campaign as defenders identify individual parts.

Persistent. Dwell time, the time it takes between the first compromise and discovery, is 95 days on average in the case of APT activity, and campaigns last longer than a year. Salt Typhoon telecom campaign was used one to two years prior to its discovery. This is a stark contrast to the median time of dwell of eight days for the general cyberattack.

Threat. APTs are structured, well-financed, human fighters who possess a certain agenda. APT groups have strategic objectives; stealing intellectual property, political espionage, sabotaging critical infrastructure, or stealing large amounts of money, unlike opportunistic cybercriminals who use what they find.

Artificial intelligence has proven to be an essential tool in detecting the existence of an Advanced Persistent Threat (APT) with capabilities to automate such processes as anomaly detection, behavioral analysis, and threat intelligence integration. Some of the AI-based APT identification methods that are discussed in this section include anomaly detection, behavioral analytics, and threat intelligence integration.

How AI Detects Advanced Persistent Threats

AI-based cybersecurity systems enable behavioral analytics, deep learning and "machine learning" (ML) to detect abnormalities, predict attacks, and automate the response of threats. AI can be used to counter APTs in the following manner:

1. **Anomalies through Behavioral Analysis.**

   Areas of conventional security that are based on rule-based detection cannot work against unknown threats. AI uses behavioral analytics to establish a point of normal network behaviour and detect abnormalities that could potentially indicate an APT attack.

   - **E.g.**, AI can identify unusual login history, unexpected data transfers, and unauthorized access attempts.

2. **Threat Intelligence and Predictive Analytics.**

   AI can be used to process large amounts of cybersecurity data, e.g., threat intelligence feeds, dark web monitoring, and attack trends, to predict such risks before they occur.

   - **Example**: To give an example, AI-based Security Information and Event Management (SIEM) systems can correlate the threat indicators of different data in real-time.

3. **Threat Hunting and Automated Incident Response.**

   AI-based technologies can be used to automate the threat hunting process, identify potential APT indicators and respond promptly to minimize harm.

- **Examples**: e.g., AI-based Security Orchestration, Automation and Response (SOAR) systems can alert security personnel, block malicious IP addresses and isolate systems that have fallen victim to attacks.

4. **Intelligent-Inspired Fraudsters.**

   AI enhances tricks used to deceive, such as decoy systems and honeypots, to lure attackers and collect information on their plans.

   - **Example:** To use an example, AI-based honeynets can trick the actors of APT into revealing their approach by dynamically adjusting to aggressive behaviour.

5. **Detection of Polymorphic Malware and Fileless Malware.**

   Advanced techniques of obfuscation and fileless malware are common with APTs. AI is capable of detecting these dangers based on a review of system behaviour, rather than relying on signs.

   - **Example:** As an example, AI-powered endpoint monitoring and response systems are used to detect and identify changes in memory and abnormal process behavior.

Techniques and Algorithms Used by AI for APT Detection

AI effectively detects and minimizes APTs using a range of techniques and algorithms:

- **Machine Learning Algorithms:** Data patterns and anomalies are found using methods including supervised learning, unsupervised learning, and reinforcement learning. While unsupervised learning finds hidden patterns without predetermined labels, supervised learning trains models using labeled datasets.
- **Deep Learning Models:** Neural networks are used in deep learning, a kind of machine learning, to examine complicated data sets. These algorithms are useful for identifying complex

APTs because they can find complex patterns in massive amounts of data.

- **Natural Language Processing (NLP):** NLP is a natural language processing that analyzes textual data, e.g., malicious code or phishing email, to determine linguistic patterns indicative of an APT activity.
- **Ensemble Methods:** By utilizing the advantages of various algorithms, combining several machine learning models (ensemble approaches) can increase detection accuracy.

Benefits of Using AI for Mitigating APTs

AI can help mitigate APT in a number of ways.

- **Improved Detection Accuracy:** AI improves detection accuracy by analyzing vast volumes of data and identifying subtle patterns that may indicate an APT.
- **Faster Reaction Times:** Automated AI systems can significantly reduce the time between detection and mitigation by responding to threats instantly.
- **Reduced False Positives:** AI models can lower false positives by accurately distinguishing between permissible activities and potential risks, allowing security professionals to focus on actual threats.
- **Scalability:** Because AI systems can expand to handle enormous volumes of data and network traffic, they are suitable for companies of all sizes.

Challenges and Limitations of AI in APT Mitigation

Although AI is beneficial, it does have several challenges in regard to APT mitigation:

- **Data Quality:** AI requires quality data in order to detect accurately. Unfinished or noisy data may negatively influence the work of AI models.

- **False Positives and Negatives**: Even with the capability of reducing false positives, AI might still generate false negatives, thereby leaving certain APTs undetected.
- **Complexity:** Implementation and management of AI systems may be a challenging task requiring special knowledge. The implementation of AI within the existing infrastructure can be a challenge to organisations.
- **Changing Dangers:** Because APT strategies evolve, AI models have to be able to adapt to different approaches all the time. A major concern that should be addressed is to ensure that AI systems are informed with the latest threat intelligence.

27. ETHICAL AND SECURITY RISKS OF AI IN DEFENSE

In cybersecurity and defense systems, Artificial Intelligence has been employed, and this has significantly transformed how organizations determine, assess threats and respond accordingly. The AI-driven systems offer speed in decision-making, real-time tracking, and large datasets processing, which make them highly effective in combating the existing threats of cybercrime. However, as systems become more autonomous and integrated and become heavily embedded in the critical infrastructure, novel types of ethical and security challenges are being introduced that cannot be disregarded.

The question is to strike a balance between the benefits of AI and potential risks. Despite the fact that AI enhances efficiency and scalability, there are also complex ethical issues that are related to privacy, fairness, accountability, and transparency. In the meantime, AI systems are also vulnerable to cyberattacks or may be used by malicious individuals to perpetrate more sophisticated and large-scale attacks. The risk environment of AI can be dynamic and challenging due to the potential of AI as an offensive weapon and a defensive mechanism.

Furthermore, the usage of AI in the military is on the increase, which means that one should consider its long-term implications. Partiality in the decision-making process, lack of explainability, overreliance on automation, and the threat to physical security are some of the issues that make it obvious why the implementation of AI should be held accountable. Therefore, to create robust, trustworthy, and responsible cybersecurity systems, one will have to be aware of ethical and security risks that AI could suggest.

Ethical risks of Ai in Defense

1. **Trade-offs in Privacy and Security:** Privacy versus security is one of the most outstanding ethical issues surrounding AI-powered cybersecurity. The use of AI poses a concern regarding privacy to the user because it is capable of analyzing large amounts of data. Consider a network intrusion detection system, which monitors the activity of users on the basis of artificial intelligence. Even with doubtful activity found, in case online activities are actively monitored all the time and all the time, this might be termed as excessive surveillance.

    - **Scenario:** In the case of the company applying AI-based network monitoring, the essential information about employees is accidentally recorded in the frame of regular monitoring. It is hard to balance security and privacy as the system must be modified to gather as little personal and other non-work-related information as possible, and be able to identify threats.

2. **Implementation of bias and fairness:** AI systems often reflect the data that it is trained on, which presents a moral dilemma of discrimination and fairness. An AI-based approach on cybersecurity may be biased and unfairly target or profile certain populations. As an example, an AI-based malware detection system can identify software that is disproportionately used by specific demographics, which can be ethically questionable due to being discriminatory and biased.

    - **Case study:** Due to the biases in the training data, a cybersecurity program will think that a valid software that is most commonly used by a particular cultural group is malicious. This raises questions of fairness and the probability of unfair and disproportionate actions and consequences.

3. **Responsibility and Decision-Making:** AI in cybersecurity can independently make its decisions, including quarantining files or blocking IP addresses. These automated processes are liable to failure, and therefore, the question of responsibility arises. This brings up serious concerns about responsibility in case AI systems are coming up with wrong results.

   - **Scenario:** An AI-based firewall blocks a vital network service accidentally and has a severe impact on the company. It is challenging to establish accountability since both the AI system and the human operators who installed and maintained it are not assessed in determining their behaviour.

4. **Transparency and Explainability:** The second ethical dilemma is that some AI models are black box systems. The reasons behind the decisions of most AI algorithms, especially the deep learning models, are hard to articulate as the basic programming and logic behind these systems are usually closely guarded intellectual property. This lack of transparency in cybersecurity can instill mistrust and doubt because security experts might not be able to understand why a particular activity was deemed harmful by AI.

   - **Example:** In case an AI system raises a red flag over a possible risk, a cybersecurity analyst would be required to explain his or her decision to act. They struggle to justify their future moves to stakeholders, however, since they cannot explain to the stakeholders clearly the reasons behind why the AI made that conclusion.

5. **Job Displacement and Economic Impact**: Due to the AI being able to automate routine threat detection, the cybersecurity industry might face job displacement. In addition to the short-term concerns of cybersecurity professionals, this ethical dilemma has more broad implications on society, including the need to retrain and reskill and economic impacts.

   - **Examples**: To use an example, a company minimizes the need of human analysts by introducing an AI-driven automated incident response. Dealing with the repercussions of potential layoffs and ensuring those affected find an opportunity to change jobs and participate in retraining is an ethical issue.

Security Risks of AI in Defense

1. **Emerging AI-Powered Attack Vectors:** New AI-Augmented Attack Vectors: Hackers can turn the same AI-enhanced defenses into an attack with more sophisticated and evasion-resistant attack forms. The biggest concern is the arms race between offensive AI and defensive AI.
2. **Adversarial Attacks and Model Poisoning:** AI models can also be attacked by generating inputs that can cause a trained model to err in its classification of data, or during training, by providing bad data, a process known as model poisoning. This can lead to failure in the identification of threats by AI systems or worse, the systems can misinterpret harmless activities as harmful. The dependability of AI-driven security systems is compromised by such attacks.
3. **Automated Malicious Tools and Campaigns:** AI is capable of automating the development and implementation of highly customized and potent cyberattacks. This includes sophisticated scanning tools, self-propagating worms, and autonomous malware that adjusts to defenses. These AI-powered attacks are extremely challenging to fight against because their speed and scope greatly exceed those of human attackers.
4. **AI-Driven Phishing and Deepfake Attacks:** For use in sophisticated phishing and social engineering efforts, generative AI can produce incredibly convincing deepfakes that are realistic but fake images, audio, or video. It is practically impossible for humans to determine the legitimacy of these AI-generated fakes since they can effectively mimic executives or reliable people. This greatly raises the likelihood that such dishonest attacks will be successful.

Risk Mitigation Strategies for AI Systems

Although AI is an effective tool, there are certain cybersecurity dangers associated with it. To utilize the technology responsibly, both individuals and organizations need to adopt a comprehensive and proactive strategy.

The following tactics can lessen the dangers connected to AI systems:

- **Regular Auditing of AI Systems**

  To prevent security and privacy concerns, find out the current reputation of any AI system you utilize. To fix vulnerabilities and lower AI threats, organizations should audit their systems on a regular basis. Experts in artificial intelligence and cybersecurity who can perform system reviews, vulnerability assessments, and penetration testing can help with auditing.

- **Limiting Sensitive Data Exposure**

  More people are using artificial intelligence to share private information without realizing the privacy risks. For instance, it was discovered that employees of well-known companies were entering private company information into ChatGPT. Unaware of the ChatGPT security issue, even a doctor entered his patient's name and health status into the chatbot to create a letter.

  Such activities violate privacy laws like HIPAA and present security dangers. Conversations are recorded for quality control and are available to system maintenance staff, even if AI language models might not be able to reveal information. Because of this, it's important to refrain from giving AI any personal information.

- **Data Security and Integrity**

  As previously stated, AI's ability to produce quality results depends on its training data. AI can provide unanticipated and hazardous outcomes if the data is altered or contaminated. Organizations must invest in state-of-the-art encryption, access control, and backup technology to safeguard AI against data poisoning. Firewalls, intrusion detection systems, and complex passwords should all be used to secure networks.

- **System Maintenance and Updates**

  To safeguard yourself against the risk of AI, adhere to all software maintenance best practices. This will require the use of the latest patches and updates to your operating systems, applications, and AI software and frameworks to reduce the chances of exploitation and malware attacks. Install the current antivirus software to protect your systems against advanced, aggressive attacks. In order to reinforce your defenses, invest more in network and application security.

- **Model Hardening and Adversarial Training.**

  Adversarial training is an AI-specific security solution that can help AI to react to threats. The machine learning approach makes AI models resilient to different scenarios, data, and techniques.

- **Training and Awareness of** the **employees.**

  The threats of AI are very diverse. In order to educate your personnel in AI risk management, make use of cybersecurity and AI experts. As an example, students would like to understand how to check the validity of emails that can be phishing attacks developed by artificial intelligence. They are also to avoid downloading unsolicited software, which may be malware that is artificially created through artificial intelligence.

- **Vulnerability Management**

  Companies can avoid risks of information leakage and data security breaches through investment in AI vulnerability management. Vulnerability management is an inclusive procedure that incorporates detection, appraisal, and ranking of vulnerabilities and reducing your attack surface with respect to the unique nature of AI systems.

- **Incident Response Planning**

  Due to the growing number of threats posed by artificial intelligence, your company might fall victim to cyber security attack on artificial intelligence despite having the most robust protection measures in place. The only way to get out of such an event is to have a clear incident response plan that discusses the aspects of containment, investigation, and remediation.

Best Practices for Responsible AI Deployment

A cybersecurity professional has to work with cyber threats and AI problems, which pose challenging and unending ethical problems. The list of the best practices that will help to negotiate this challenging landscape and use AI successfully without violating ethical norms is presented below.

- **Explainability and Transparent Communication:** Communication of a transparent nature is important. A cybersecurity expert can be very important in his or her organization by making sure that he or she informs all stakeholders of the capabilities and limitations of an AI system. Such transparency will inspire trust and dispel any concerns about the black box/AI component.
- **Detection and Reduction of Bias:** Be on the lookout for biases in the AI systems and respond to them accordingly. This involves advocacy of inclusive and diverse sources of data, betterment of models to reduce bias and frequent auditing of training data. The elimination of bias is one of the ways to ensure that AI-based decisions are appropriate and just.
- **Development of Accountability Frameworks**: Development of clear accountability frameworks is important. Identify the person in charge of AI-based decisions and activities through close work with the legal and compliance departments. This should be defined and determined during a deployment as soon as possible. Such clarity helps in resolving conflicts and ensures that there is the sharing of responsibility in a proper manner.
- **Continuous Education and Ethical Training:** It is important to keep abreast with the latest developments in AI ethics.

Lifelong learning helps to gauge the ethical AI issues and adjust the strategies to align with varying standards.

- **Data Custodianship and Data Security:** To balance the level of privacy and security needs of the users, develop strict data handling practices. This involves only collecting information that is necessary, anonymizing of sensitive information and avoiding unwanted access to data by encrypting and control of access to data.
- **Regular Auditing and Reviewing Ethics:** It is important to conduct regular audits on AI systems. With the help of these evaluations, necessary changes can be made to maintain ethical standards, and new ethical topics can also be revealed.
- **Collaboration and Engagement with the AI Society:** It is actually helpful to collaborate with the greater community of AI. The most effective methods of dealing with ethical considerations in AI may be located through sharing knowledge and insights.

By adhering to these best practices, cybersecurity professionals can maintain the uncomfortable balance between using AI in cybersecurity and observing moral norms. Ethics and surveillance are still needed as cybersecurity and AI are continuously changing. A cybersecurity professional has the responsibility of protecting the ethical integrity of any AI-driven defenses, besides system and data defense.

28. INDUSTRY IMPLICATIONS OF AI-DRIVEN DEFENSE

The defense sector is quickly undergoing change due to Artificial Intelligence, which presents a new wave of automation, intelligence and strategic input. The capabilities being improved through AI-driven systems include cybersecurity, threat detection, autonomous cars, and surveillance. To process large amounts of information in real-time and make decisions faster and more precisely, machine learning algorithms are relying on them increasingly in defense organizations. This change reduces the human error in situations that involve high stakes, and the operational efficiency is greatly enhanced.

The consequences of AI integration into the defense sector are wide-ranging to the defense sector and the related industries. The firm engaging with defense production is shifting towards creating smart systems, such as autonomous drones, intelligent weapons, and predictive maintenance solutions. This is leading to the investment of more in research and development and also the cooperation of governments, private technology companies, and research centers. This is causing the traditional defense ecosystem to become more technology-oriented and an innovative industry.

Nonetheless, the application of AI in defense raises some critical moral, legal, and financial concerns, as well. Issues such as data safety, responsibility in making independent decisions, and the likelihood of abusing the AI technologies are significant problems. The possibility of an AI arms race between countries makes the global security situation even more complicated, which may result in global instability and the rise of geopolitical tensions. Also, the issue of the displacement of the workforce exists since automation will render some jobs unnecessary in the domain of defense.

In spite of these issues, AI-based defense systems have long-term returns such as, superiority in national security, cost-effectiveness and better strategic flexibility. The governments and leaders in the industry should focus on ensuring that effective legal frameworks and moral standards are established to ensure that AI is used appropriately. By balancing the responsibility with innovation, the defense sector will have the full use of AI and minimize the associated risks, in the end resulting in a safer and technologically better future.

Technological Transformation in the Defense Industry

The use of artificial intelligence in defense systems is radically transforming the technological environment in the industry. The systems that are being substituted with intelligent data-driven systems with autonomous functions are the mechanisms that have been heavily dependent on human decision-making and manual operations. Machine learning, computer vision and natural language processing, similar to

AI technologies, are facilitating advanced surveillance, real-time threat analysis and predictive intelligence. These features enable the defense forces to handle high levels of information from various sources, such as satellites, drones and communication networks, among others and greatly improve situational awareness and efficiency in operations.

In addition, AI innovations are making it faster to develop autonomous weapons systems, so-called unmanned aerial vehicles (UAVs), and robotic ground systems. Such technologies lessen the reliance on the human factor in areas of high risk thus reducing casualty counts and enhancing the success rate of the mission. The move to software-defined defense systems also promotes continuous upgrades and flexibility, whereby military capabilities can keep up with the new threats. Consequently, the defense sector is no longer a hardware-focused environment but a more flexible and technology-driven ecosystem.

The other notable feature of the technological revolution is the incorporation of AI into the prevailing defense infrastructure. Existing systems are being enhanced to have smart functionality so that there is a smooth interaction between the older hardware and new software-based systems. As an example, command and control systems that are enhanced with AI have the potential to synchronize numerous defense assets in real-time, enhancing reaction time to critical operations. The digital twins and simulation technologies also enable the defense organizations to test strategies and project the consequences before executing them in real-world settings and scenarios.

Moreover, edge computing and real-time analytics are also improving the functionality of AI-based defense systems. AI models can work directly on devices like drones and surveillance devices, instead of sending data to a centralized data processor. This minimizes latency and guarantees quicker decision-making in time-sensitive scenarios. With more changes in these technologies, the defense-related industry is set to realize greater autonomy, accuracy, and flexibility, and this is likely to redefine contemporary warfare and defense mechanisms.

Economic and Industrial Impact of AI Integration

The introduction of AI in defense is influencing a major shift in the economic framework and industrial forces in the industry. The defense organizations are also making more investments in research and development in order to be competitive in a rapidly changing technical environment. Consequently, this has created additional market opportunities for technology firms, startups, and cybersecurity companies to build a collaborative ecosystem between the public and the private sector. There are also instances where large defense contractors are entering into strategic alliances with AI-oriented businesses to develop innovations faster and shorten the development cycle.

Simultaneously, the workforce required is becoming more and more professional and in especially in data science, AI engineering, and cybersecurity. Though AI opens new employment opportunities, it also disfigures the conventional roles, which cause labor market change and require reskilling and upskilling programs. Moreover, AI-based automation helps to optimize costs due to operational efficiency, lessening maintenance costs because of predictive analytics, and simplifying supply chain management. Such economic changes are transforming the nature of the defense industries in terms of operation, competition and long-term growth.

The emergence of AI in defense also has an impact on the world's supply chains and defense procurement plans. Governments are also putting more emphasis in national manufacturing of important technologies in order to cut down on the reliance on external suppliers in order to boost national security. This trend is spawning the emergence of domestic industries and centers of innovation to work on AI and defense technologies. Concurrently, there is the emergence of international collaboration and joint ventures that are enabling the nations to exchange experience, resources and technology development whilst making control and risks manageable.

Moreover, the economic effects of the implementation of AI are not limited to direct operational advantages. Investments in AI-based systems in the long term are projected to pay off significantly in terms of increased efficiency, decreased downtime, and increased rate of mission success. Nonetheless, the initial implementation costs are very high, and the system requires continuous upgrades, which is why it is difficult to allocate budget and plan the financial expenditures. The dilemma of innovation versus cost management is one of the most important issues that have been considered by policymakers and leaders in the industry as they grapple with the changing landscape in the defense arena.

Ethical, Legal, and Strategic Challenges in AI-Driven Defense

Although it has several merits, there are Multifaceted ethical, legal, and strategic challenges associated with deploying AI in defense systems. One of the primary concerns is the usage of autonomous weapons, where the responsibility and judgment in matters of life-or-death situations are challenged. The question of who is responsible for the behaviour of AI systems remains an important issue, especially in cases where some unforeseen consequences are experienced. Moreover, the possibility of AI technologies being used with bad intentions, e.g., cyberwarfare and autonomic attack, is a serious threat to international security.

Laws and global policies are finding it difficult to keep up with the speed of innovation of AI in defense. Lack of universally accepted standards would bring about uncertainty and make it harder to avoid the emergence of conflicts due to the unregulated use of AI. Also, more dependence on AI systems creates data privacy vulnerabilities, system integrity and cybersecurity threats. Strategically, the emergence of AI-powered defense features can result in an arms race between states, which will escalate the level of geopolitical tension. Such problems require a balanced approach involving the application of ethical governance, international cooperation, good policy formulation, and technical innovation (Emmanuel, 2026).

Multiple Choice Questions (MCQs)

1. **What is the primary purpose of AI-driven threat detection systems?**

   A. To replace human analysts completely

   B. To detect and respond to threats in real time

   C. To increase network traffic

   D. To store large volumes of data

2. **Which of the following is a key advantage of using Machine Learning in cybersecurity?**

   A. Eliminates all cyberattacks

   B. Requires no training data

   C. Identifies patterns and detects unknown threats

   D. Works only on structured data

3. **Behavioral analytics in cybersecurity mainly focuses on:**

   A. Hardware performance

   B. User and system behavior patterns

   C. Network cables

   D. Software installation

4. **Anomaly detection is used to:**

   A. Block all network traffic

   B. Identify deviations from normal behavior

   C. Encrypt sensitive data

   D. Increase system speed

5. **What does SOAR stand for in cybersecurity?**
   A. System Operations and Risk
   B. Security Orchestration, Automation, and Response
   C. Secure Online Access Resource
   D. Software Optimization and Analysis Report
6. **The main function of SOAR platforms is to:**
   A. Replace antivirus software
   B. Automate and coordinate incident response processes
   C. Increase manual workload
   D. Store backup data
7. **Advanced Persistent Threats (APTs) are characterized by:**
   A. Short-term attacks
   B. Random hacking attempts
   C. Long-term, targeted attacks
   D. Physical system failures
8. **How does AI help in defending against APTs?**
   A. By ignoring network traffic
   B. By detecting hidden patterns and continuous monitoring
   C. By deleting all data
   D. By slowing down systems
9. **Which of the following is a major ethical risk of AI in defense systems?**
   A. Increased electricity usage
   B. Bias in decision-making algorithms
   C. Faster processing speed
   D. Better data storage

10. **What is a key challenge of using AI in cybersecurity?**
    A. Lack of internet
    B. High cost and adversarial attacks on AI models
    C. Too many employees
    D. Limited storage space

Answers

1	2	3	4	5	6	7	8	9	10
B	C	B	B	B	B	C	B	B	B

Chapter 5

FUTURE DIRECTIONS IN CYBER RISK MANAGEMENT

29. OVERVIEW

The evolving technology and the sophistication of cyber threat is making cyber risk management take a different turn. The conventional reactive security model is obsolete in the scene where the attackers have evolved and automated, in most instances, and are driven by artificial intelligence. Organizations are increasingly becoming more proactive and predictive to detect threats before they turn into reality, so that they can use advanced analytics, machine learning, and threat intelligence to detect threats. Such a transition can be applied to enhance the rapid detection, rapid response time and a hard, resilient security posture (Gerstein & Leidy, 2024).

The other important tendency is the spin of the former one, and it is the introduction of cyber risk management as a part of the general enterprise risk and governance processes. Cybersecurity is gradually becoming a business necessity, as opposed to a pure technical issue. These involve introducing in-line risk management practices whose organizational goals, regulatory standards and industry standards. The postulates on the rise are zero trust architecture, constant observation, and measurement of risks that assist organizations in making informed decisions and distributing resources in a better way to accommodate the arising threats.

Furthermore, there is a future with the focus on teamwork, automation and people-centric security policies. Due to the complexity and growth of cyber-attacks, organizations are investing in automated response and orchestration tools that will minimize human error and enhance efficiency. Simultaneously, cybersecurity, training, and culture are given more attention as it has already been acknowledged that human behavior is one of the crucial key points of management regarding risk. Technology innovation and informed individuals would help the organizations build a nimbler and more resilient defense against the emerging threats in cyberspace through the sharing of information in an alliance.

30. ZERO TRUST ARCHITECTURES

Zero Trust Architecture (ZTA) is currently the model of the modern approach to cybersecurity that rests on a general philosophy, which is never trust, always verify. Unlike the classical security models, which assume that everything inside the perimeter is secure, ZTA offers a default of untrustworthiness to all users, devices and applications, in and out of the network.

The approach is the ongoing verification and authentication of all the access inquiries and minimizes the attack domain, sideways movement and protects the significant assets in an extremely distributed digital setting.

Key Points

- **Only Credit What You Can Weigh:** ZTA is founded on a philosophy that it is essential to never trust implicit trust and that all requests to access must be treated as threats, no matter the source.
- **Always Verify:** All attempts to access are verified, authorized and validated in accordance with all existing data points and an ongoing verification process.
- **Micro-segmentation:** ZTA provides granular network segmentation to allow only the exact resources required, minimizing the blast radius of the potential breach heavily.

- **Least Privilege:** This concept guarantees the user and devices to be assigned no more than the minimal necessary access to complete their particular tasks.
- **Assume Breach:** ZTA works on the premise that a breach has occurred and constructs security controls to harness and manage those threats that have already gained access to the network.

The transformation to cloud services, remote working, and hybrid IT deployment has made the concept of perimeter security an outdated occurrence. Workers operate in any location. The applications reside in more than one cloud. Devices, some of which are not managed, access through the firewall. The result? A constantly widening attack surface.

Zero Trust Architecture comes into play as a strategic response to this new normal by:

- Substituting blind trust with dynamic and contextual verification.
- Limiting access to curb harm in case of an intrusion.
- Offering uniform security between hybrid and multiclouds and on-premises.

The Core Tenets of Zero Trust

The zero-trust security model is composed of the basic principles according to which an organization handles network access and data protection. ZTA isn't a product. It is the mentality that is supported by certain security principles. Here are the non-negotiables:

- **Never Trust, Always Verify**

  Implicit trust is entirely removed and is the most basic principle of a Zero Trust model. This implies that the default assumption is that no user, device or workload may be trusted even prior to connecting to the corporate network.

  Any access request should be validated and verified, no matter whether it is created within or outside the traditional network perimeter. This constant checking procedure makes sure that a compromised entity cannot move freely all over the network.

- **Least Privilege Access**

  The least privilege principle provides that a user or a device receives the minimal amount of access necessary to fulfill his or her designated role. This minimizes the blast radius of breach and the exploit that attackers can do.

- **Assume Breach**

  Zero Trust is based on the belief that a breach is neither possible nor an eventuality. This assumes breach mindset compels security teams to come up with controls that have the potential to constrain threats that have already evaded the preliminary controls.

  Rather than emphasizing perimeter protection, the emphasis is on in-house monitoring, detection of threats and prompt action to halt the lateral movement and reduce the effects of the breach.

- **Context-Sensitive Access Policies.**

  The decisions made on zero trust access are never fixed but are dynamic and made based on diverse contextual information. These policies examine the identity of the user, the security posture of the device, the position of the request and the sensitivity of data accessed.

  One such policy may be to bar access to sensitive financial information when the user is trying to access it via a public Wi-Fi network, despite the correct credentials.

- **Microsegmentation**

  The networks are isolated into zones to eliminate lateral movement. Although an attacker may hack one segment, he or she cannot move freely in the environment.

  The Zero Trust security model is built on fundamental principles that govern how an organization approaches network access and data protection. ZTA isn't a product.

The Benefits of Zero Trust Architecture

The application of ZTA will provide contemporary businesses with a more secure and flexible environment. It has some major advantages even in the environment of changing cybersecurity threats:

- **Improved Security:** ZTA lowers the attack surface by providing least privilege access and continuous authentication that denies unauthorized users access to sensitive data.
- **Defense against Data Breaches:** With the authentication involved in each request, ZTA reduces the chances of a data breach even in the case a device in the network is breached.
- **Greater Visibility and Monitoring:** The model depends on constant monitoring and logging, which leads to better visibility of an organization, which is more effective in its response to threats.
- **Less Exposure to Advanced Persistent Threats (APTs):** Isolating network segments and performing access validation at every tier means that ZTA reduces the effects of advanced lateral movement-based attacks.
- **Scalability:** ZTA is simple to scale to support the increasing user base, device count, and applications, which means that it is appropriate to use it by both large and small businesses. Remote Work and Cloud Environment Support: ZTA can be used to support remote workers and multicloud environments in a secure way, and provide secure access to any location.
- **Meets Compliance Needs:** ZTA complies with regulatory data protection laws, such as GDPR, HIPAA, and PCI-DSS.

How Zero Trust Architecture Works

Zero Trust Architecture is not a single technology, but rather a unified system or structure created by a combination of various interdependent security elements. Its essence is built on an all-inclusive strategy to network, identity, and device security. It demands a policy engine to implement access decisions based on continuous verification and validation.

- **IAM Identity and Access Management.**

  The pillar of Zero Trust is identity. The model should have a wholesome IAM solution capable of validating the identity of each user and application trying to gain access to the resource. These would encompass powerful authentication techniques, which include multifactor authentication (MFA) and single sign-on (SSO). It is also important to authenticate the identity of non-humanized objects, e.g. APIs and machine identities.

- **Microsegmentation**

  Microsegmentation refers to the act of cutting a network into small and non-interconnected segments all the way to the individual application workload. It enables security teams to develop access policies, which are resource-specific and accurate, with the help of this granular segmentation. When a threat breaches one of them, it cannot spread to other segments, which is a kind of containment of the breach and limits its effects.

- **Posture Validation and Device Security.**

  The identity of the user is as insignificant as the integrity and security of a device. Zero Trust entails constant verification of the posture of devices, such as installing up-to-date operating systems, firewalls, and malware-free.

  In case a device is reported to be non-compliant, it can be quarantined or denied access to corporate resources until the problem has been resolved.

- **Live Intelligence and Analytics.**

  The principle of always verifying needs continuous monitoring. ZTA platforms are used to derive real-time network traffic, user logs and device logs analysis with the help of advanced analytics and cyber threat intelligence.

31. QUANTUM COMPUTING AND CRYPTOGRAPHIC RISKS

Quantum computing is a threat to current cybersecurity because it is simply based on the fact that modern cryptographic systems are created by the mathematical principles on which modern cybersecurity is implemented on attack systems. Quantum computers cannot be likened to classical computers that handle information using bits, which can be expressed in the form of 0s or 1s, but the qubits, which can be expressed in a multiplicity of states concurrently, by the law of superposition. There is also entanglement between qubits, and the state of a single qubit is proportional to the state of the other qubit, although there might be physical distance between them. The properties permit the quantum systems to compute in radically new ways from the way in which classical computation is performed.

This computing capability has some wonderful implications for encryption. They are also used in classical systems in a series manner to test potential solutions, and this makes certain mathematical problems computationally infeasible to find solutions within a reasonable time. Rather, quantum computers can search multiple solutions simultaneously, which has a strong potential of improving processing efficiency. It is this parallelism that enables quantum systems to discover patterns and solutions significantly quicker than traditional machines, thereby putting the security assumptions of widely-used cryptographic algorithms into question.

Most of the secure communication in the contemporary world is founded on the symmetric cryptography algorithms: RSA, elliptic-curve cryptography (ECC), and Diffie-Hellman (DH). These are founded on the difficulty of mathematical problems of factorization of large integers and discrete logarithms. These issues would impractically consume a lot of time on the limits of classical computing, which ensures the safety of encrypted information, the use of digital signatures, and authentication systems. This complexity is, however, reduced to a small fraction by quantum computing algorithms.

An excellent example, which can compromise the security of popular cryptosystems based on the public-key algorithm, is the Shor algorithm, which can factor large numbers exponentially faster than the classical algorithms. This presents an immediate challenge to privacy and the integrity of information since the derivation of the private keys can be attained within a reasonable time. Similarly, the algorithm invented by Grover also influences symmetric cryptography, the change in which is to accelerate the process of brute force search, thus reducing the actual security of the encryption schemes. Symmetric key lengths would need to be significantly increased so as to guarantee the same degree of security.

As quantum computing advances further, it will necessitate the transition to quantum-resistant or post-quantum cryptography. To begin preparations for this transition, organizations must first review the current cryptographic system and adopt algorithms that are resistant to quantum attacks. The emergence of quantum technologies indicates that the aspect of urgency is important in reevaluating the existing security models to ensure that data is safeguarded in the long-term in a more sophisticated computational environment.

Cybersecurity Risks Introduced by Quantum Computing

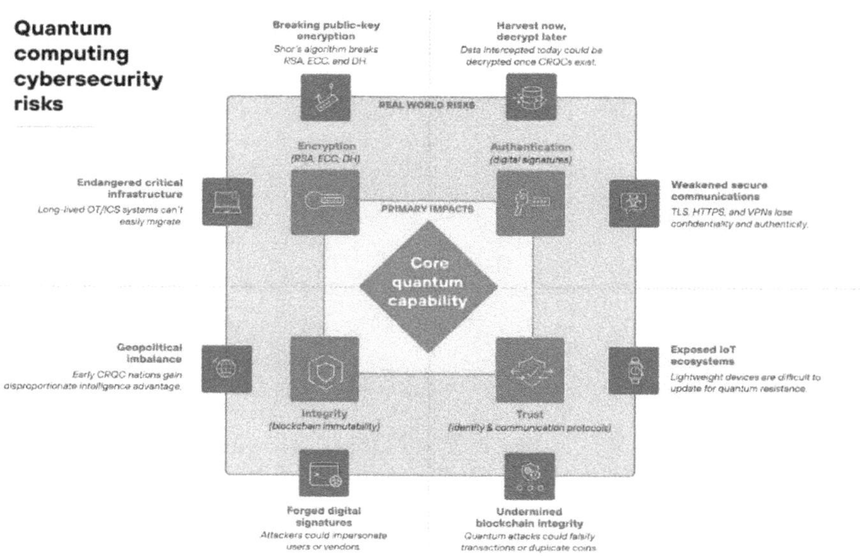

Figure 5.1: Quantum Computing Cybersecurity Risks

The greatest threats posed by quantum computing are its effects on cryptography, which secures virtually any digital system.

In other words, all these risks are based on a single fundamental characteristic: the power of a strong quantum computer to solve some math problems much faster than classical ones.

These risks go all the way to encryption and authentication to national security.

Here's what that means in practice.

1. **Breach of the public-key encryption.**

   Quantum computers would be able to use the algorithm of SHOR to factor large integers and compute discrete logarithms efficiently. That is a direct attack on RSA, elliptic-curve cryptography (ECC), and Diffie-Hellman (DH).

   With the existence of a CRQC, the integrity of the keys used to encrypt traffic, the digital signatures as well as the authentication systems may all be compromised.

2. **Encrypting stored information at a later point in time (harvest now, decrypt later).**

   Hackers are now able to intercept encrypted traffic and store it to decrypt it at a later stage. That stored information can be decrypted in a short time when quantum computers are developed.

   This creates a delayed risk. Since the sensitive data that has been deemed secure for decades could be readable overnight when quantum capability is finally developed.

3. **Hacking of digital signatures and identity verification.**

   Integrity and authenticity are verified by the use of digital signatures. Assuming that quantum computers can obtain the private keys, they will be able to generate the signature that will seem legitimate.

That would enable malicious users and actors to masquerade as trusted software vendors or users.

4. **Making blockchain non-integrity.**

   The majority of blockchain systems rely on ECC in order to verify transactions.

   Quantum attacks would allow the users to alter transactions or clone coins. Such violates the permanence on which blockchain relies, endangering cryptocurrencies and any distributed ledger-based enterprise system.

5. **Sabotaging secure communications.**

   Some of the technologies, such as TLS, HTTPS, VPNs and email encryption, are based on the principle of a public key exchange to achieve trust.

   The outcome is the loss of confidentiality and authenticity of traffic, endpoints and credentials on inter-global systems of communication.

6. **Exposing IoT ecosystems**

   The Internet of Things devices frequently employ lightweight encryption, which is also efficient, in contrast to quantum-resistance.

   They are also hard to maintain after being deployed. This is particularly susceptible to post-quantum exploitation of large, distributed networks of the IoT.

7. **Endangering critical infrastructure**

   Long-lived keys and cryptography keys are usually used in operational technology (OT) and industrial control systems (ICS). These systems cannot be upgraded quickly.

   The problems may be on quantum attacks that can threaten key industries such as energy, healthcare, and transportation in case migrations fall behind.

8. **Establishing geopolitical disequilibrium.**

   The CRQC capability will be disproportionately useful in intelligence and defense to the first nations or organizations to develop their capability.

   Diplomatic, military, and economic information of other countries could be leaked in the form of encrypted data. Such an imbalance can transform world politics over the internet.

Post-Quantum Security: Organizational Preparedness and Emerging Challenges

Most organizations are still in the early stages of preparing for a post-quantum future. But the transition has begun.

Quantum readiness is now being treated as a multiyear program, not a single upgrade.

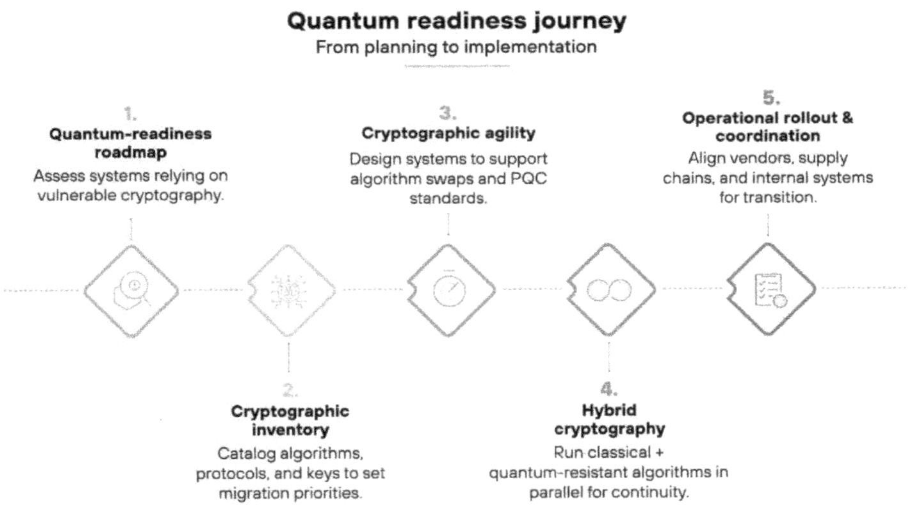

Figure 5.2: Quantum Readiness Journey

Here's what that looks like.

There are numerous business ventures that begin with quantum-readiness roadmaps.

This is the plan of which systems are based on vulnerable cryptography and how they will ultimately transition to quantum-safe systems.

CISA and other authorities would suggest starting with a cryptographic inventory.

This is done by indexing all the algorithms, protocols and keys being used so as to establish migration priorities according to risk exposure.

The second one is cryptographic agility.

That implies the ability to create systems that are responsive enough to replace algorithms with new standards. It is one of the main components of the preparation of the final standards of NIST on the post-quantum cryptography (PQC), which will require years to be fully adopted in terms of software, hardware, and cloud platforms.

There are also others that are trying out hybrid cryptography.

That is a mixture of classical and quantum-resistant algorithms in the transition phase to retain backward compatibility.

There are challenges to consider, though.

- Many organizations are becoming increasingly conscious with disproportionate urgency. They, too, are aware of the danger but rely on vendor road maps before committing. That causes delays, particularly to the large organizations with entrenched systems.
- Meanwhile, smaller organizations often have to use upstream providers, such as cloud or hardware vendors, to do the transition on their behalf.
- Another problem is the supply chain. Although an enterprise may upgrade its own systems, this may not be the case with its partners or vendors. Such interdependence implies that one frail link can bring the risk back towards the end of migration.

In general, the Global Risk Institute discovered that there is a wide range of preparation among sectors, with few organizations having formal quantum-transition plans.

Ultimately, it is not only cryptography that is being thus far in a post-quantum security race. It's about coordination. And in the case of most organizations the work must begin today in order to be ready when the standards are.

Building Blocks of Quantum-Safe Cybersecurity

The future of cybersecurity is taking a rapid turn towards quantum-safe systems that would be counter to attacks that are both classical and quantum. With the development of quantum computing, companies can no longer afford to consider it a far-off risk but a change that cannot be overlooked and that must be prepared for within a short period of time. The second step in cybersecurity is to establish resilient, layered systems that combine various technologies to provide protection of data over time and operational security.

The most fundamental component of this change is post-quantum cryptography (PQC), which is a counterpart to quantum-safe security. PQC substitutes weak public-key algorithms with new quantum-resistant cryptographic algorithms that are based on mathematical problems. The current state of standardization has already achieved much success with NIST completing major PQC standards like ML-KEM, ML-DSA and SLH-DSA under FIPS 203 up to 205 with additional algorithms such as FN-DSA (FALCON) anticipated to be added. The developments offer a systematic way of enabling organizations to start migrating towards quantum-resistant systems.

Nonetheless, PQC is not enough in order to cover the entire range of emerging risks. These are the complementary technologies that are being incorporated to enhance the security framework. Quantum Key Distribution (QKD) is a system used to facilitate the exchange of keys safely as quantum mechanics are used to monitor any attempts of eavesdropping in real time. Equally important, Quantum Random Number Generators (QRNGs) also make cryptography more powerful because they produce true randomness and there is no predictability in the key generation. The combination of these technologies brings important levels of confidence, especially where the incentives are critical like in the world of finance, defense, and telecommunications.

In order to facilitate a seamless process, a lot of organizations are embracing hybrid cryptographic strategies that incorporate both classical and post-quantum algorithms. The approach provides support of backward compatibility with current systems with the gradual deployment of quantum-resistant mechanisms. Hybrid models minimize the threat of disruption and enable businesses to upgrade their infrastructure without interfering with the current operations.

Simultaneously, governance, testing, and certification frameworks are being created in order to provide the reliability and standardization of quantum-safe implementations. Technology vendors, governments and industry groups are putting funds in automated test tools, compliance programs and deployment guidelines to hasten the adoption. Furthermore, companies are doing cryptographic inventories and using crypto-agility frameworks, which allows them to adapt rapidly to changing standards and threats.

All in all, quantum-safe cybersecurity is not a theory but a reality that is being actively implemented. As the global cybersecurity ecosystem continues to invest, collaborate and innovate technologically, the basis of a secure quantum-resilient future continues to be established.

32. CYBER INSURANCE AND FINANCIAL RISK TRANSFER

Since cyber threats are only getting more and more frequent and affecting organizations in a greater scale, cyber insurance is becoming a key element of organizational risk management. Predefined traditional security controls prove to be not effective and do not slow down the effects of sophisticated cyberattacks that include ransomware, data breaches, and cases of business interruption as a whole. Cyber insurance provides a financial bailout, which enables organizations to transfer some percentage of their cyber risk to the insurers and be confident that in case of any unforeseen interruption, they will still have business continuity.

The cyber insurance policies are also so constituted that they can expand the range of losses that they are able to cover through incident response, legal liabilities, regulatory fines, and reputational damages. Such a form of financial risk transfer will help the organizations be better placed to respond to the economic repercussions of the cyber incidents that would otherwise cause colossal operational and financial liability. Due to this, organizations are not just spending money on preventive measures to protect against cybersecurity but also making their insurance policies more consistent with the wider enterprise risk management models.

In addition, the increasing need for cyber insurance is pushing organizations to embrace intense security measures, with insurers pushing to have stringent risk evaluation and adherence to cyberstate regulations before the issuance of cyber insurance. This changing dynamic between insurers and organizations is contributing to an increasingly active attitude towards cybersecurity, which involves collaboration between financial protection and technical resilience to deal with the intersecting and shifting aspects of cyber threats.

Working of Cyber Insurance

The process of cybersecurity insurance takes place similarly to insurance policies. Many suppliers offer policies that sell other types of business insurance, including errors and omissions insurance, liability insurance and property insurance. Cyber insurance policies will either cover first-party coverage, which is a loss that directly affects an enterprise, or third-party coverage, which is a loss incurred by other enterprises that have a business relationship with the affected organization.

Cyber insurance policy assists an organization to pay all the financial losses that they might suffer due to a cyberattack or data breach. It also assists them in covering any costs associated with the remediation process, including the money spent on the investigation, crisis communication, legal services, and customer reimbursements.

Scope of Coverage in Cyber Insurance

Cyber insurance coverage may differ depending on the requirements of the business, data types that are kept by the business and the industry in which the business lies. Various cyber policies have both first-party and third-party cover options. The first-party coverage covers direct losses of the business, such as the cost of data recoveries and reinstating systems. Third-party coverage gives coverage of damage to the parties to the business, such as consumers who have had theft of their data.

In terms of certain losses, many cyber policies cover such items as:

- **Business interruptions**

  In case a firm loses income due to the fact that a cyber-attack puts the computer systems offline, there is a possibility that cyber policies would cover a portion or all of the losses.

- **Remediation and threat response.**

  Responding to an incident, repairing the system, and conducting a forensic investigation and other services required following a cyber event may be covered by insurance.

- **Legal expenses**

  Cyber policies can be used to cover costs of litigation in case of a cyberattack, including customer litigation. Certain insurance corporations can provide the insured company with legal representation.

- **Data breach recovery**

  In the event that hackers steal personally identifiable information (PII) or any other sensitive data, including credit card or social security numbers, cyber policies may be used to pay the expenses of notifying the customers and offering such services as credit monitoring.

- **Regulatory action**

  Cyberattacks can result in regulatory inquiries, particularly within highly regulated sectors, such as the healthcare industry and the financial sector. Cyber policies can reimburse the expenses of fulfilling such audits, as well as fines that the company has to pay.

- **Reputation management**

  The company's stance could require employing a PR company or other measures to salvage its brand after being attacked. Certain cyber policies will be used to offset these costs.

- **Ransom payments**

  Most cyber policies also include ransomware payments; however, due to the high cost of ransom, there are insurance providers ceasing or reducing this coverage.

Typical cyber insurance exclusions

Although cyber policies may be comprehensive, there are incidents that they will not cover. These are called exclusions. Common exclusions include:

- **Breaches of third parties**

  When vendors and other partners are hacked, a company can lose the data it keeps or have its services interrupted. These losses are not always covered by cyber insurance; however, certain insurers will provide third-party breach coverage at an extra cost.

- **Social engineering**

  Since social engineering attacks, such as phishing tricks, are tricks that play with human beings to undermine cybersecurity in the interiors, such losses are not always covered by cyber policies. Nevertheless, social engineering coverage can also be purchased as an optional one.

- **Insider threats**

  Insider attacks, such as malicious or careless employees, are insurance risks that are hardly covered.

- **State-sponsored attacks**

  Such attacks are seen as an act of war and will not be addressed by many cyber policies.

- **Ransomware attacks by a known vulnerability.**

  When a flaw is hacked by hackers and the company is aware of it, but fails to rectify it, an argument will be rejected by many cyber policies.

- **Cyberattacks are not the reason behind network failures.**

  It is rare to see most plans cover outages due to misconfigurations and other internal errors.

Key Methods of Risk Transference

1. **Cybersecurity Insurance**

   Most of the most frequent risk transference is done via specific cybersecurity insurance cover. These policies are to pay financial losses caused by data breaches, ransomware attacks, business interruptions and other cyber-related issues.

   Types of Coverage:

   First-party coverage: Covers first-party losses to your organization.

   - Response and notification costs of a data breach.
   - Business interruption losses.
   - Digital asset restoration
   - Cyber extortion payments

   Third-party coverage: covers against claims of other people.

   - Privacy liability
   - Network security liability
   - Media liability
   - Regulatory defense costs

2. **Service Level Agreements (SLAs) and Contracts.**

   Some of the risks can be assigned to vendors and service providers by organizations with well-developed contractual agreements:

   - Indemnification provisions: Demand that vendors pay your organization because they cause it to suffer losses.
   - Limitations of liability clauses: Capped financial liability.
   - Security requirements: Requirement of certain security controls to be upheld by vendors.
   - Breach notification requirements: Be aware of events in time.

3. **Managed Security Service Providers (MSSP).**

   Another useful risk transference method is to outsource security services to security service providers:

   - 24/7 security monitoring
   - Incident response services
   - Threat intelligence
   - Vulnerability management

   When organizations collaborate with MSSPs, they alleviate the operational risks incurred in running complicated security infrastructure and staffing security departments.

4. **Cloud Service Providers**

   The transfer of operations to a reputable cloud platform shifts part of the infrastructure security risks:

   - Physical data center security.
   - Patching and updating platforms' security.
   - Network security controls
   - Has adhered to industry standards.

   But it is important to realize the shared responsibility model, where, though providers have secured the infrastructure, you are still liable for data security and access controls.

Best Practices for Effective Risk Transference

1. **Perform Serious risk analysis.**

   Before you transfer any risk, you have to know what you are transferring:

   - **Identify valuable assets:** Decision on what should be guarded.
   - **Gauge threats and vulnerabilities:** Learn what can go wrong.
   - **Measure possible effects:** Estimate possible losses in terms of such methodologies as Annual Loss Expectancy (ALE).

   Prioritize risks: Always concentrate on those risks that have a high impact with high likelihood.

2. **Choose the appropriate Insurance Cover.**

   It is important to work with well-learned insurance brokers. The most common advice on Reddit was that the trick is to find an agent/broker who specializes in cyber (there are a few who do it well).

   When evaluating policies:

   - **Coverage to your risk profile:** Make sure that the policy covers your threats.
   - **Learn exceptions and requirements:** Learn what is not covered.
   - **Check incident response services:** Check the quality of the provided services.
   - **Check over claim:** Learn what you are going to need to be documented.
   - **Think regulatory concerns:** Make sure that the policy assists in complying with regulatory requirements.

3. **Bargain Firm Vendor agreements.**

   In case of risk transfer to vendors:

   - **Identify security responsibilities:** Specify security ownership.

- **Add security policies:** Requirement security controls based on policies.
- **Create the right-to-audit clauses:** Have transparency into vendor security.
- **Specify the periods of incident notification:** Proceed with timely knowledge of breaches.
- **Ensure the cyber:** and insist on the vendors being insured.

4. **Document Everything**

   Keep detailed records of all claims that can be made:

   Security controls inventory: Procedure in all the safeguards in place.

- **Evidence of compliance:** Keep Compliance records.
- **Security testing outcomes:** Document penetration tests and vulnerability analysis.
- **Incident response plans:** Document and conduct periodic tests of procedures.
- **Training records of employees:** Security awareness program attendance.

33. WORKFORCE DEVELOPMENT AND CYBER TALENT STRATEGY

With cyber threats becoming more complex and widespread, companies are becoming more aware that technology in itself cannot provide a high level of security without a talented and dynamic workforce. The development of the workforce has become a vital aspect of the cybersecurity strategy because it is associated with the development, maintenance and upskilling of talent to handle the dynamic threat environment. This need is only enhanced by the cybersecurity professional deficit that afflicts the world in general, and it makes organizations reevaluate the means through which they can lure and nurture talent in the highly competitive environment.

The overall strategy of cyber talent is to pay attention not only to hiring special professionals but also to internal institutions on the basis of the training and education programs. To ensure that the employees remain in a place where they can handle the emerging threats, companies are investing in continuous learning programs, qualifications and practical simulation. Secondly, the cross-functional training is also gaining importance, because the non-technical staff is familiarized with the basics of cybersecurity and assists in the creation of an information security culture within the organization.

The other significant factor is the relevance of the workforce strategy to organizational goals and risk management focus. This is achieved through the identification of the major positions, the development of skill requirements, and the creation of a defined career laddering among the cybersecurity practitioners. With the implementation of the talent strategy aligned with the business needs, the organizations will be in a position to make sure that the workforce is technically competent and can make strategic decisions that would enable the overall resilience building.

Moreover, cyber talent development of the future focuses on diversity, teamwork, and automation. The increase in the talent pool through the different approaches employed to promote diversity in participation contributes to the diversity of thinking to the problems at hand, and the cooperation between the academic, industry and the government aids in the creation of useful skills and knowledge. Meanwhile, the process of automation and artificial intelligence implementation is transforming the role of the workers and providing professionals with an opportunity to devote their energy to more strategic activities. These measures combined can help organizations develop an adaptive and resilient cybersecurity workforce in the future.

Skill Development and Continuous Cybersecurity Training

This is because the environment associated with the cyber threats is rapidly changing and as such, constant acquisition of competencies in the cybersecurity workforce is a prerequisite. The obsolete one-time training is no longer available since new vulnerabilities; methods of attacks and technologies are discovered at an unprecedented pace.

The organizations must be capable of adopting dynamic approaches in learning techniques to ensure that employees are constantly updated on the latest information and applicable skills that help them fight against any type of modern cyber threat.

The positive attributes of the ongoing training programs are the ability to train the cybersecurity personnel in technical skills. These programs typically contain certifications, workshops, online classes and hands-on laboratories, which mimic a simulated attack setting. The professionals will have the opportunity to understand the behavior of the threat and become more prepared to respond to the stressful circumstances with the help of practical activities, such as penetration testing and incident response simulation.

Other than the technical training, there is also the interdisciplinary learning which organizations are presently putting emphasis on. The issue of cybersecurity has stopped being an issue in the IT departments; it cuts across business processes, legal business operations, and risk management. This causes the employees in different functions to be inspired to develop a rudimentary understanding of cybersecurity principles. This is the global perspective wherein security issues are put into consideration in every organizational decision.

Moreover, the introduction of novel technologies, such as natural intelligence and automation, is transforming the requirements in skills. In order to protect the data, computer experts now have to master analyzing data, intelligence of threats and automated security applications.

Talent Acquisition and Retention in Cybersecurity

As the demand of cybersecurity skills surpasses their supply, companies are competing in their endeavors to acquire skilled individuals. This has witnessed the emergence of new sources of recruiting, which include academic institutions, participation in cybersecurity competitions, and the use of specially-crafted training programs to identify and nurture new talent in a bid to discover and develop new talent.

It is also necessary to retain talent in addition to hiring professionals. This failure to retain in the cybersecurity occupations can cripple the operations of a business and expose more vulnerabilities to an organization. To cope with this, organizations are striving towards the creation of good working environment that gives good remuneration, promotion and recognition of input. Career development and advancement also help in ensuring that the employees remain interested and committed.

The other distinction of talent strategy is the workforce that has been diversified. Inclusion of people with diverse backgrounds and experience, such as non-traditional career lines, will help expand the talent pool and add a new dimension to solving problems. Besides boosting creativity and innovation, diversity enhances an ability of a given organization to solve complex and multifaceted cybersecurity challenges.

Additionally, another way of addressing the problem of skills shortage is the development of talent in companies through investment by the companies themselves. It may be a cost-effective and sustainable solution comprising of training the existing employees and enabling them to change their careers to cybersecurity roles.

Building a Security-Aware Organizational Culture

Even though the use of the newest technologies and qualified specialists is also crucial, the issue of human behavior can be ranked among the most significant aspects that predetermine the outcomes of security. The staff are typically at the frontline of the fortification and their ideas and actions may either stop or cause a security event.

The awareness measures that the organizations are supposed to encompass in their activities should also be wide-ranging to the extent that they enlighten the employees on the common cyber threats, such as phishing, social engineering, and malware. These programs are expected to be amusing and relevant in such a way that the employees will be in a position to recognize and respond in case of a threat in a real-life situation. The regular training and simulated phishing activities, along with awareness campaigns, can also be used to increase the level of employee vigilance significantly.

The culture of security is quite essential and the leadership assists in the attainment of the same. Once the top management appreciates cybersecurity and leads by example by supporting best practices, it leaves its footprint and encourages the staff to take security seriously. It can be made to be a priority of each and every tier of the organization by including cybersecurity in company policies, performance rates, and daily routine and underline the importance of cybersecurity.

Besides, a high security culture is accountability and improvement-oriented. Organizations are urged to promote the open discussion of security incidents, near-misses and use them as a learning experience rather than blaming other people. This is not merely a better method of reaction to incidents, but it also creates trust and collaboration between colleagues. Lastly, good security culture will assist organizations to remain on the offensive of risk management so that it can stand strong in a threat environment that is increasingly becoming complex.

Workforce Planning and Role-Based Cybersecurity Governance

Good workforce planning is vital in trying to match the capabilities of cybersecurity and the organizational goals and risk priorities. Cyber threats are increasingly becoming more advanced; therefore, it is necessary that the right individuals with the right capabilities be placed in the right positions. It will involve the definition of core cybersecurity functions, role-specific roles, and matching skills requirements with the organizational requirements. A planned workforce is useful in a more effective manner in distributing resources and efficient and responsive security operations.

Role-based cybersecurity governance additionally underlines this approach because the role-based governance presents highly distinct levels of accountability at the organizational level. The current organizations distributed the tasks of cybersecurity across various departments instead of having all the responsibilities of cybersecurity by having the entire responsibilities under one team. This entails distribution of responsibilities; the responsibilities that are distributed include security analysts, incident responders, compliance officers, and risk managers, whose responsibilities are clearly defined. Such clarity will reduce the confusion in case of occurrence and the response will be faster and more organized.

Additionally, the tendency is also shifting towards homogenous organizations to shape the planning and control of staff. The role-based access control (RBAC) and cybersecurity competency models are models that help to ensure good practices and provide employees with the right access and duties. The frameworks are also useful in compliance to the regulatory provisions and best practices in the industry which adds credibility and trust to the organizations.

Finally, it is important to have an operational planning of the workforce through continuous review and changes. As the environment of the threat and technologies change, organizations must also re-evaluate the period of their labor, redefine functions, and address new skill gaps. A combination of workforce planning and governance mechanisms allows organizations to build a more resilient, accountable and future prepared cybersecurity workforce.

34. BUILDING ADAPTIVE AND RESILIENT CYBER ECOSYSTEMS

Organizations must cease to use a transactional security framework and begin to build dynamic and robust cyber ecosystems in a time that is defined by rapidly changing cyber threats and increasing digital interconnectivity. The previous type of perimeter-based defenses is not efficient in a world where data, applications and users are distributed in distributed networks. Cyber ecosystem approach has concentrated on interconnection practice, intelligence sharing as well as a continuous process of adapting of systems to be able to effectively withstand, respond and recover to disruptions.

Contemporary approaches to the problem of cybersecurity rely heavily on flexibility. The high-level and dynamic mode of attack by the threat actors will require organizations to develop systems that learn and can adapt to them in a timely manner. This is also associated with integration of modern technologies such as artificial intelligence, machine learning and automated threat detection systems. Such tools provoke the anticipatory actions of vulnerability and faster response to incidents, reduce the potential impact of cyberattacks and enhance the overall system agility.

The other is resilience, which is involved with the continuity of operation in adverse conditions. This can be brought about through resilience by ensuring that backup systems are robust, redundancy is in place, and there are disaster recovery measures that would ensure that business-critical functions are in place after and during a cyber incident. It further requires that organizations should be risk-based and be concerned with safeguarding critical assets and make recovery operations highly effective and well-coordinated.

Besides, the development of a strong cyber ecosystem is premised on collaborating and integrating the stakeholders. Governments, technology providers and private organizations have to work together to offer threat intelligence, establish common standards and make improvements on common defenses. By cultivating the culture of continuous improvement and teamwork, the organizations will be able to create a cybersecurity environment that will not only be reactive to the evolving threats but also proactive and robust.

Key Components of the Cyber Ecosystem

An effective cybersecurity plan must acknowledge the following important elements of the cyber ecosystem:

1. **Participants**

   Examples include:

   - **Individuals and Users:** Clients and consumers who rely on digital services.
   - **Organizations:** Private companies, government agencies, non-profits, etc.
   - **Cybersecurity Teams:** Professionals responsible for protecting digital assets.

2. **Processes**

   Critical processes include:

   - **Incident Response:** The process of identifying, analyzing and eliminating cyber-attacks.
   - **Risk Management:** Ongoing evaluation, analysis and reduction of possible risks.
   - **Compliance and Audits:** Ensuring operations meet regulatory standards like GDPR, HIPAA, etc.

3. **Data**

   Data is both an asset and a liability:

   - **At Rest:** Data stored on disk drives or cloud storage.
   - **In Transit:** Data moving across networks; encryption is vital here.
   - **In Use:** Data actively processed by applications, which requires robust protection using access controls.

4. **Technologies**

   Technological components include:

   - **Hardware:** Devices that process, store, and transmit data.
   - **Software:** Operating systems, applications, and security tools.
   - **Cloud Services:** SaaS, IaaS, and PaaS platforms forming a significant part of modern cyber ecosystems.
   - **Zero Trust Network Architecture:** A paradigm requiring strict verification for every person or device attempting to access resources.

5. **External Environment**

   Factors outside of organizational control:

   - **Regulatory Constraints:** Laws and policies dictate how data should be handled.

- **Market Pressures:** Evolving customer demands for secure and accessible digital services.
- **Global Cyber Threat Landscape:** International cybercrime trends and new attack strategies that can affect local organizations.

Adaptive Security Mechanisms and Technologies.

Cyber threats are dynamic and changing thus, adaptable security measures are needed to counter cyber threats. Unlike the traditional security models, which are founded on fixed security solutions, the adaptive security is founded on continuous monitoring and real-time analysis and an automatic response. In this, the organizations would be in a position to detect anomalies which may lead to dangerous situations at their initial stages and respond before it is too late to respond. Adaptive security augments the efficacy of the cybersecurity strategies by transforming to the predictive model to the reactive model.

The main characteristic of promoting adaptive security is the use of new technologies, such as artificial intelligence (AI) and machine learning (ML). These technologies analyze huge amounts of data to define the pattern, abnormal behavior and potential threat. To illustrate an example, anomaly detection systems can detect deviation of normal user activity and predictive analytics can be utilized to anticipate attack vectors in the history. It is at this level of intelligence that the organizations will be able to stay ahead of attackers and continually work on their defenses.

Automation is the other valuable feature of adaptive security. Security orchestration, automation and response (SOAR) systems make the process of incident response easier by automating the monotonous task of managing the incident, such as identifying the threat, assigning alert priorities, and responding to the incident. This will not only save the response time, but will also minimize the number of human errors, and this will imply that cybersecurity units will be dealing with more complex and strategic issues. The automation is also the means of providing that security measures can be further developed according to the complexity of organizational systems.

Moreover, the feedback should be continuous in order to improve the adaptive security. Frequent reconsideration of security stance by companies, updating their signaling, and putting into practice the lessons in the past cases should be taken into consideration. It is a continuous process that has to update the security systems to keep abreast of the new, constantly changing threats and emerging threats. Adaptive security mechanisms are an effective and versatile defense framework of intelligent technologies, automation, and ongoing learning to defend the contemporary cyber ecosystem.

Cooperation and Exchange of Intelligence on Threats in Cyber Ecosystems.

They rely on co-operation and sharing of threat intelligence as the solution to enhancing resilience to manage cyber ecosystems in the ever-linked digital reality. The cyber threats are likely to cross organizations, industry and geographical borders, and it is difficult to address them on an individual basis. Through sharing threat intelligence, the organizations can have access to useful information about the emerging threats, attack patterns, and vulnerabilities, and can have more knowledgeable and effective countermeasures.

Examples of threat intelligence dissemination are the exchange of information (in terms of indicators of compromise (IOCs), malware signatures, and attack techniques). Formal networks, industry alliances and government-led programs are usually considered as the means in which such information is exchanged. With the help of such coordination systems, the organizations will be better placed to build up their situational awareness and respond more appropriately to potential threats. The threat intelligence is made available early enough and this is what helps organizations to ensure preventive measures are taken first before the attacks can get into their systems.

Social cooperation between the government and companies is another significant matter of increasing cybercrime resilience, besides official cooperation. Governments are often involved in providing regulatory support, a feeling of threat intelligence and incident response, but the technical aspect and field experience are provided by private organizations. The cooperative strategy has helped in the development of a coordinated defense strategy, which helps to ensure that the critical infrastructural support and vital services are more resistant to cyber threats.

In addition to this, the sharing of intelligence is impossible without a culture of trust and cooperation. Companies must be in a position to devise secure methods of communication, standard procedures and elucidated policies that can embrace the transmission of sensitive information. The competition and the data privacy problems are significant barriers that could be conquered to achieve maximum benefits of cooperation. Lastly, the consistent approach to disseminate threat intelligence can enhance the well-being of the whole cyber system and make the entire cyber ecosystem more resilient.

35. INDUSTRY TRANSFORMATION AND FUTURE READINESS

The situation of cyber risk has changed with the dynamic digitalization of all industries. The attack surfaces grow with the adoption of new technologies, such as cloud computing, artificial intelligence, and the Internet of Things (IoT) and blockchain in organizations. This has increased interdependency and reliance on electronic systems and hence introduces new threats; therefore, cyber risk management is an essential part of strategic planning. The future is no longer a matter of choice but rather a necessity and organizations that want to continue in business and be an assured player in an ever-digitized economy.

The paradigm shift within the industry should imply the transition of the previous risk management strategies to the new, more coordinated and active approaches to cybersecurity. We are also witnessing organizations and companies incorporate an element of security in their central business procedures and ensure that an element of security is considered at each level of digital innovation. This incorporates the implementation of models that promote ongoing risk evaluation, real-time tracking and response systems. With the adaptation of the business goals to cybersecurity, the organizations can reduce risks and make expansion and innovation safe.

Introducing resilient and flexible infrastructures is the other significant indicator of preparedness of the future. Due to the constantly changing environment of cyber threats, organizations must be positioned to recover and overcome disruptions and respond quickly to events. This incorporates the adoption of sound back-ups, disaster recovery and redundancy procedures that will not result in disruption in operations. In addition, the concept of cyber resilience is concerned with the ability to learn and continually improve security practices, which enables organizations to change their security practices, depending on the evolving threat environment.

In addition, the collaboration and regulatory congruence also play a vital role in the creation of an industry-wide preparedness. Governments and individual organizations are working together with regulatory bodies in developing standards, threat intelligence sharing and best practices. Compliance with the evolving regulations also enhances security, besides building confidence between the stakeholders. Having an innovative, strong and collaborative culture, organizations will have a chance to bargain the dynamics of the cyber risk and find their place in a safe and sustainable future.

Digital Change and Growing Cyber Risk Environments.

In cloud computing, remote working patterns and the networked digital platforms, digital transformation has become one of the unique aspects of modern enterprises. Despite the fact that such developments are beneficial in terms of efficiency in operations, innovation at the same time, it leads to a significant rise of cyber risk environment. With the growth of the number of organizations that become more digital in their operations, the number of potential entry points of cyberattacks also grows, and the concept of perimeter-based security becomes less and less relevant.

The change involving the distributed systems and cloud-based infrastructure has led to a boundary ambiguity on the fact that sensitive data is not only in one environment. This complication is a problem of visibility, similar to and comparable to security policies that are difficult to handle. Moreover, the risks are also increasing because there is a high dependency on third-party vendors and supply chain partners, as any vulnerability of one partner may be transferred to the others parts of the ecosystem.

The driving forces of the increasing cyber risk environment include:

- Additional hybrid environments and cloud services are being used.
- IoT-related proliferation of connected devices.
- Development of homework and mobility.
- Greater dependence on third-party supply chain and vendors.

This compels organizations to be more holistic and integrated on cybersecurity because risk is no longer confined to the organizational boundaries anymore but it is distributed throughout a complex and interdependent digital ecosystem.

New Technologies and the Implications to Security

The future technologies that are transforming the industries, but also introduce new security threats to the existing ones, are artificial intelligence, blockchain, quantum computing, and the Internet of Things. These technologies are revolutionary, and they also create new attack vectors that the current security systems have not yet been equipped to deal with completely. The organizations, which are to stay on top of the evolving cyber threats, should integrate the understanding of their implications.

An example is artificial intelligence, which can be employed to find and counter threats more efficiently and enhance security by automated attack detection and defending against enemies, which can also be automated by the enemy to produce advanced phishing attacks and bypass the more conventional methods. Additionally, there is minimal or no protection available on IoT devices and that would imply that they are easily susceptible to hackers who do not hesitate to exploit poor security. As discussed earlier, quantum computing would pose a threat to the implemented cryptographic systems in the long run and thus necessitates the application of quantum-resistant algorithms.

The new technologies have significant security implication of:

- The integrated and distributed systems result in exposing the system to a greater attack surface.
- Difficulties in the resource-seeking of devices with limited resources, such as IoT endpoints.
- The employment of AI to cause high-tech and automated cyberattacks.
- The threat of quantum computing to break the existing cryptographic standards.

To manage these companies should address the issue of security when they are designing and implementing new technologies. This incorporates the application of secure-by-design, comprehensive risk evaluation and continuous tracking of the technological development in such a way as to anticipate the threats in the future.

Strategic Readiness and Cyber Resilience to the Future.

As cyber threats keep evolving, organizations must be strategy-ready and resilient in order to be in a position to sustain themselves in the long run. The issue of future readiness is not only the development of sophisticated security technologies but also a systematic association of cybersecurity and business strategy, risk management, and organizational culture. It is a hybrid system that assists organizations in anticipating any potential threat and responding to any disruption.

Cyber resilience puts emphasis on the ability to withstand, to adapt or to bounce back to cyber incidences. This requires a high level of security control, well defined incident response procedures and regular tests of recovery procedures. The companies should abandon the idea of a prevention-based approach and change to the vision of the unpreventable breaches and emphasize prompt identification and recovery.

Strategic preparedness and resilience consist of the following major components and consists of:

- Enforcement of zero trust system and continuous monitoring.
- Lay out response and disaster recovery plan.
- Governance structures and cyber risk assessment.
- Employee training and security awareness.

Last, in order to develop a resilient cybersecurity posture, an attitude towards it must be proactive and responsive. Organizations can easily sail through the complexities of the dynamic threat environment and be ready to live with a secure and resilient future through good governance culture and innovative technological implementation.

MULTIPLE CHOICE QUESTIONS (MCQS)

1. **What is the main goal of cyber risk management?**

   A. Eliminating all cyber threats

   B. Managing and minimizing risks to acceptable levels

   C. Ignoring low-level threats

   D. Increasing system complexity

2. **What does a Zero Trust Architecture (ZTA) primarily assume?**

   A. All users are trusted by default

   B. Internal networks are always secure

   C. No user or system should be automatically trusted

   D. Only external users are threats

3. **Which principle is central to Zero Trust Architecture?**

   A. Trust but verify

   B. Verify explicitly and continuously

   C. Open access policy

   D. Shared credentials

4. **How does quantum computing pose a risk to cybersecurity?**
   A. It slows down encryption processes
   B. It can break traditional cryptographic algorithms
   C. It reduces computing power
   D. It eliminates malware

5. **Which type of cryptography is considered resistant to quantum attacks?**
   A. Symmetric cryptography
   B. Classical RSA encryption
   C. Post-quantum cryptography
   D. Hash functions only

6. **What is the purpose of cyber insurance?**
   A. Prevent cyberattacks
   B. Transfer financial risk associated with cyber incidents
   C. Replace cybersecurity tools
   D. Eliminate legal compliance

7. **Which factor is crucial for effective cyber risk management workforce development?**
   A. Reducing employee training
   B. Ignoring skill gaps
   C. Continuous learning and upskilling
   D. Limiting access to tools

8. **What is a key challenge in cyber talent strategy?**
   A. Excess of skilled professionals
   B. Rapidly evolving threat landscape requiring new skills
   C. Low demand for cybersecurity jobs
   D. Over-automation of systems

9. **What defines an adaptive and resilient cyber ecosystem?**
   A. Static security policies
   B. Ability to respond and recover quickly from threats
   C. Complete isolation from networks
   D. No dependency on technology

10. **Which approach helps organizations prepare for future cyber risks?**
    A. Ignoring emerging technologies
    B. Relying only on traditional defenses
    C. Integrating innovation with proactive risk management
    D. Avoiding investment in cybersecurity

Answers

1	2	3	4	5	6	7	8	9	10
B	C	B	B	C	B	C	B	B	C

BIBLIOGRAPHY

1. Ali, S., Wang, J., & Leung, V. C. M. (2025). AI-driven fusion with cybersecurity: Exploring current trends, advanced techniques, future directions, and policy implications for evolving paradigms– A comprehensive review. *Information Fusion, 118*, 102922. https://doi.org/10.1016/j.inffus.2024.102922

2. Barakat, A. (2025). AI-driven threat intelligence: Strengthening cyber defense mechanisms in international cybersecurity frameworks. *International Journal of Science and Research Archive, 14*(3), 598–615. https://doi.org/10.30574/ijsra.2025.14.3.0722

3. Emmanuel, E. J. (2026). *AI-powered cybersecurity innovations for protecting U . S . critical infrastructure. 29*(February), 81–92.

4. Farzaan, M. A. M., Ghanem, M. C., El-Hajjar, A., & Ratnayake, D. N. (2025). AI-Powered System for an Efficient and Effective Cyber Incidents Detection and Response in Cloud Environments. *IEEE Transactions on Machine Learning in Communications and Networking, 3*(May), 623–643. https://doi.org/10.1109/tmlcn.2025.3564912

5. Ganguli, V. G., & Contributors, S. (2024). *Securing Digital India Against AI & Cyber Threats Leveraging AI Security & Zero Trust.*

6. Gerstein, D. M., & Leidy, E. N. (2024). *Emerging Technology and Risk Analysis.*

7. Ovabor, K., Sule-Odu, I. O., Atkison, T., Fabusoro, A. T., & Benedict, J. O. (2024). AI-driven threat intelligence for real-time cybersecurity: Frameworks, tools, and future directions. *Open Access Research Journal of Science and Technology, 12*(2), 040–048. https://doi.org/10.53022/oarjst.2024.12.2.0135

8. Shrivastav, A. (2025). AI-Driven Cyber Defence for India's National Security. *Electronic Journal of Social and Strategic Studies, 06*(07), 139–171. https://doi.org/10.47362/ejsss.2025.6608

9. World Economic Forum. (2025). *Artificial Intelligence and Cybersecurity: Balancing Risks and Rewards.*

ABOUT THE AUTHORS

Shaikh Ahmed is a Senior Cybersecurity Engineer with over 14 years of experience in identity and access management (IAM), privileged access management (PAM), cloud security, and enterprise infrastructure protection. He has worked with leading organizations including Truist Bank, Delta Air Lines, and Tata Consultancy Services (TCS), securing large-scale environments and driving compliance and data protection initiatives.

He holds industry certifications including CompTIA, is an IEEE member, and actively contributes to the cybersecurity community through peer reviews, judging, conference speaking, and published articles. Through his work, Ahmed focuses on building secure, scalable systems and advancing modern cybersecurity practices.

Shaikh Irfan is a cybersecurity professional specializing in vulnerability management, threat detection, and security operations. With over six years of experience, he has secured large-scale enterprise systems using tools like Splunk, Qualys, and Tanium.

He holds the CompTIA Security+ certification, is an IEEE member, and has been recognized with the Global Infosec Award. Through his writing, Irfan aims to simplify complex cybersecurity concepts and make them practical for real-world use.

www.ingramcontent.com/pod-product-compliance
Lightning Source LLC
LaVergne TN
LVHW051051210926
848486LV00002B/72
* 9 7 9 8 9 0 4 5 1 5 8 7 4 *